JOIN the CONVERSATION at
#1010LIFE

Visit Pastor Daniel Hill's blog at
PASTORDANIELHILL.COM

Follow him on
TWITTER @DANIELHILL1336

D0009656

10:10

LIFE

TO THE FULLEST

DANIEL HILL

BakerBooks

a division of Baker Publishing Group
Grand Rapids, Michigan

Published by Baker Books
a division of Baker Publishing Group
P.O. Box 6287, Grand Rapids, MI 49516-6287
www.bakerbooks.com

Printed in the United States of America

Library of Congress Cataloging-in-Publication Data is on file at the Library of Congress, Washington, DC.

ISBN 978-0-8010-1629-5

Published in association with the literary agency of Mark Sweeney & Associates, Bonita Springs, Florida 34135

14 15 16 17 18 19 20   7 6 5 4 3 2 1

*To my community of brothers and sisters
at River City Community Church:
thank you for helping me experience firsthand
the fullness of life in Christ.
I wouldn't be who I am without you.*

Contents

Foreword by John and Nancy Ortberg   11

Acknowledgments   13

Part 1 Something's Missing

1. The Emperor Is Naked   17
2. Something's Missing   24
3. People of the Story   30
4. Faith in 3-D   41

Part 2 Faith and Fear

5. The Great Command   51
6. Boundary Breaking   61
7. Sink or Swim   71
8. Safe or Brave   78
9. Pay Attention   88

Part 3 Faith and Intimacy

10. The Center of Faith   99
11. The Garden   110

12. Independence Day   121
13. The Butterfly Effect   131
14. Pleasing God   141

Part 4 Faith and Mission

15. Mission Impossible   153
16. Lord of the Harvest   165
17. Kingdom People   176
18. Witness   185
19. Neighbors   199
20. Fully Alive   211

Notes   219

Foreword

Meeting Daniel close to fifteen years ago and now reading his words on these pages is so congruent.

The same passionate, scrappy, and dedicated man we knew then comes through now on the printed page. Even back then, during our times at Axis, Daniel was both living and exploring what it meant to follow Jesus and find the abundant life he offered. We think the words in this book can help you do the same.

Daniel came to realize the role that fear plays in limiting our faith, our vision, and our ability to live life to the fullest. Fear, in all of its forms, is so insidious. By design, we are tempted to overlook, avoid, or dismiss it. We become so unaware of the deep and invasive ways that fear permeates our lives. That posture makes it impossible for faith to grow. The kind of courage it takes to plumb the depths of your own fears is a rare thing indeed. Watching Daniel resolutely do just that was and is nothing short of inspiring.

Daniel's story is our story. From his personal life to his corporate and now ministry life, he beckons us to this intersection of fear and faith, telling us it's safe and necessary to be there. Throughout this book, you will find memorable and penetrating insights that will linger in the mind and lodge in the soul. These words will help guide your own journey through fear to faith. Diving deeply into Scripture, Daniel reminds us of the many places we see God recognize and address fear in his people when they are blind to it. He shows us the many ways in which God opens our eyes and beckons us to walk away from the fear that is paralyzing us.

For us, what is especially powerful has been reading this book and holding it up next to Daniel's life and seeing the integrity that is there: he lives what he declares. Having known Daniel for many years—from working alongside him and watching him date and work out his singleness (there's another whole book there!) and then find his lovely wife, Liz, to seeing him carve out ministry in a tough but rewarding inner-city neighborhood in Chicago and welcome his children Xander and Gabby—we continue to be deeply moved by the way he embraces, wrestles with, and refines his faith. And now you, the reader, have the privilege of joining in community with Daniel as well as he encourages and exhorts us to live life to the fullest. How quickly the student becomes the teacher.

John and Nancy Ortberg

Acknowledgments

To Cheri Saccone and David Swanson—I could not have written this book without the constant feedback and suggestions the two of you provided.

To Elizabeth—You are the rock that lets me pursue these dreams. I'm eternally grateful for you.

To the River City leadership team—You are the place where these ideas get worked out. I remain amazed at the level of depth and insight you possess.

To my agent, Mark Sweeney—What a gift you provided by pushing me to be laser clear on what God was leading me to write.

To the Baker Books publishing team—It has been such a privilege to work alongside you on this project. Jon Wilcox, thank you for making the editing process such a life-giving journey.

Part 1

SOMETHING'S MISSING

1

//////////////

The Emperor Is Naked

It is the mark of the good fairy-story . . . that however wild its events, however fantastic or terrible the adventures, it can give to the child or man who hears it, when the "turn" comes, a catch of the breath, a beat and lifting of the heart.

J. R. R. Tolkien, "On Fairy-Stories"

As a child I loved fables. They were short and simple, yet even when I was a kid they spoke to me. One fable that stayed with me through the years was "The Emperor's New Clothes," mainly because of the timeless lesson it embodied. Do you know the story?

There once lived a vain emperor whose primary concern in life was to dress in elegant clothes. He changed clothes almost every hour and loved to show them off to his people. His reputation preceded him, and a pair of troublemakers devised a scheme for taking advantage of the Emperor's vanity.

They came to the Emperor's guards and gave their best sales pitch. "We are two very good tailors, and after many years of research we have invented an extraordinary method to weave a cloth so light and fine that it looks invisible. As a matter of fact, it is invisible to anyone who is too stupid and incompetent to appreciate its quality."

The guards notified the Emperor, and his curiosity got the better of him. He decided to meet the two tailors and hear their pitch firsthand. Knowing of his vanity, they cleverly played his ego, convincing him that he should finance their next project: creating the most beautiful robe the world had ever seen.

The Emperor bought it hook, line, and sinker. He couldn't wait to wear this priceless robe. Of course, he convinced himself that vanity wasn't the motivation. The tailors promised that the robe would appear to be invisible to all who were stupid and incompetent. If that were true, it would allow him to discern which people in his empire were foolish and which were wise. Ultimately this would make him a better leader, right?

The true evidence of how badly the Emperor wanted this to work was seen in the immensity of resources that he poured into this project. Fine silk, gold thread, and large sums of money were consistently provided to meet the tailors' ongoing demands.

Because of the substantial investment, the Emperor figured he should send his old and wise prime minister to check in on their progress. When the prime minister arrived, the two troublemaking tailors worried that he might see through their scheme. They hoped that they could avoid any suspicion by exploiting his lengthy tenure. The prime minister had an established position in the Emperor's administration, and the tailors figured he would not want to risk his position.

Before showing the prime minister the garment, they reminded him that anyone who was unable to see it would be exposed as stupid and incompetent. As they laid out the imaginary robe, the prime minister strained his eyes looking for the fabric that wasn't there. He was filled with nervousness and even embarrassment. He couldn't see the robe, but he couldn't risk appearing to be a fool. Ultimately, he commended the tailors on their fine work, then went on to tell the Emperor how amazing it was. The prime minister authorized another round of expensive gold thread to be sent to the tailors, and the Emperor agreed.

Finally, the Emperor was told that the two tailors had come to take all the measurements needed to tailor his new suit. "Come in," the Emperor ordered.

Even as they bowed, the two troublemaking tailors pretended to be holding a large roll of fabric. "Here it is, Your Highness, the result of our labor," they said. "We have worked night and day, and at last the most beautiful fabric in the world is ready for you. Look at the colors and feel how fine it is."

Of course the Emperor did not see any colors and could not feel any cloth between his fingers. Surprised and feeling somewhat panicked, he chose not to admit his inability to see the fabric, for he could not allow others to know that he was evidently stupid and incompetent. What the Emperor didn't know was that everyone around him thought and did the very same thing.

The farce continued as the two tailors had foreseen it. Once they had taken the measurements, the two began cutting the air with scissors while sewing with their needles an invisible cloth.

"Your Highness, you'll have to take off your clothes to try on your new ones." The two troublemakers draped the new clothes on him and then held up a mirror. The Emperor was embarrassed, but since none of his bystanders appeared to be, the feeling quickly subsided.

"Yes, this is a beautiful suit, and it looks very good on me," the Emperor said, trying to look comfortable. "You've done a fine job."

"Your Majesty," the prime minister said, "we have a request for you. The people have found out about this extraordinary fabric, and they are anxious to see you in your new suit." The Emperor was doubtful about showing himself naked to the people, but then he abandoned his fears. After all, no one would know about it except the ignorant and the incompetent.

"All right," he said. "I will grant the people this privilege." He summoned his carriage, and the ceremonial parade was formed. A group of dignitaries walked at the very front of the procession and anxiously scrutinized the faces of the people in the street. All the people had gathered in the main square, pushing and shoving to get a better look. Applause welcomed the regal procession. Everyone wanted to know how stupid or incompetent his or her neighbor was, but as the Emperor passed, a strange murmur rose from the crowd. Many said, loud enough for others to hear, "Look at the Emperor's new clothes. They're beautiful!" "What a marvelous train!" "And the colors! The colors of that beautiful fabric! I have never seen anything like it in my life!"

They all tried to conceal their disappointment at not being able to see the clothes, and since nobody was willing to admit his own stupidity and incompetence, they all behaved as the two troublemakers had predicted.

A young boy, however, who had no important job and would only acknowledge that which he actually saw, went up to the carriage.

"The Emperor is naked!" he said.

Those within earshot quickly grew silent. Most assumed that both the child and his parents would face punishment for speaking such heresy.

But soon that silence turned into a chorus of whispers, and the whispers finally turned into full voices. "The Emperor is naked. What the child said is true."

This was the moment of truth for the Emperor. He heard the voice of the boy and then the murmuring of the crowd, and deep down inside, he knew they were right. But if he admitted the entire process had been a charade, where would that leave his reputation in the eyes of the people? No, his pride would not allow him to concede to the reality that had now become apparent to everyone around him.

Audaciously, the Emperor straightened his back, held his head high, and proudly continued the charade.

///////////

I love this story, because it serves as a parable for the spiritual experience of many Christians. In John 10:10—a life verse for many Christ followers—Jesus proclaims that he has come to bring life "to the full." That is a promise that taps into humanity's deepest desire. It summons images of wholeness and health, abundance and adventure. It evokes a sense of potential and destiny within us.

But for a large number of Christ followers, the promise seems just beyond our reach. Too often the words that describe our faith sound more like this: *comfortable*, *safe*, *routine*, and *status quo*. Sometimes even *mundane*, *mediocre*, *empty*, and *stagnant* become the descriptors of our everyday spiritual experience.

This creates quite the dilemma. What are we to do when we believe in the beauty and presence of God but struggle to translate that belief into actual experience? Where do we turn when we feel trapped between our longing and our reality? What do we do when we have fully submitted our lives to Jesus yet still carry a gnawing sense that something is missing?

Many of us find ourselves at the same crossroads as the onlookers in "The Emperor's New Clothes." The story climaxes when the crowd comes face-to-face with the naked Emperor. He is strutting around proudly, supposedly wearing the finest garment the world has ever seen. But in reality he is wearing anything but that—he is naked!

What will the crowd do? Will they have the courage to acknowledge the obvious? Or will they hide behind their fears and insecurities? The answer, of course, is the latter. Each one sees clearly, but without fail, bravery dissipates under a cloud of fear.

What were they so afraid of? Some were afraid of looking foolish. Some were afraid of being an outcast. Some were afraid of being viewed as incompetent. Some were afraid of being "that" guy or "that" woman. Some were afraid of how the Emperor would respond. Some were afraid of how their peers would respond.

No metaphor is perfect, but I think this describes the state many Christians find themselves in. Many of us have received the free gift of grace by faith and acknowledged Jesus as the Lord of our lives. We have even experienced seasons of genuine life change. But time and trials seem to draw a curtain over what once seemed so clear to us. We now feel like something is missing.

Now comes the important part: Will we have the guts to face it, like the boy in the story who saw what was clearly missing and wasn't afraid to state the obvious? Or will we be like the crowds who went along with the illusion? Will our energy be directed toward fitting in, or will it be directed toward bravery and courage?

Fear is as real for us as it was for the crowd. All kinds of fears can paralyze our ability to bravely admit that something is still missing.

We fear that by admitting what is true we will be exposed as some type of spiritual fraud.

We fear that this admission will call into question whether we ever had faith in the first place.

We fear that people will talk about us, or worse, that we will become outcasts in our community.

We fear that God will choose not to forgive us for saying it out loud.

Some of us fear that God may not even be there and that we are just participating in some type of spiritual charade.

Perhaps the fear stems from a deep, internal anxiety. What if God doesn't love me? Or worse, what if I am not redeemable? Like the men and women in the story, we can often look around and take our cues from the crowd. We can easily think, "It seems to be working for everyone else. Why isn't it working for me? I better at least pretend it is."

Integrity is at the center of this battle, because pretending to believe the illusion further fragments us, while acknowledging the truth helps put us back together. One of the most powerful promises from Jesus is that "the truth will set you free" (John 8:32). Free from what? Free from having to sacrifice this life to a shell of what could be, rather than living out the life God has for us right now! But in order to move forward, wherever our starting point is, we must be brave enough to see the truth, tell the truth, and submit to the truth.

Whenever I would hear this fable growing up, I found myself wishing that I were like that little boy in the story—brave enough to speak the truth and say what was on my mind. Instead, I found that I was usually defined by my need to fit in. While the little boy had the courage to say what was true, I was more often gripped by fear of what truth-telling might cost me. A part of me longed to stand free and independent from the crowd. But the other part of me—the part that usually won—preferred to be like the people in the crowds who went along with the charade. In the crowd I was indistinguishable and forgettable, but at least I was safe from being exposed. That concession didn't make me feel noble, but I didn't have the guts to choose the alternative.

Decades later, I continue to be amazed at how something as simple as being honest about what you see can be so incredibly difficult. Some of us think we are better at it now that we are a bit older and wiser. But the truth is that many of us have just gotten so used to blending in that we can't tell the difference anymore. Who knows what all those people who saw the Emperor were thinking? Maybe they didn't trust what they saw and figured they had to go with the wisdom of the crowd. Maybe they did trust what they saw but feared the consequences of telling the truth.

The boy in this story reminds us that in order to acknowledge the truth, we must be brave. It takes courage to truly see, to truly hear, and to truly absorb the reality of who we are. It takes courage to see what this world is and who God is. But when we step bravely into the area that unsettles us, we position ourselves to experience God for who God truly is. It is in those unsettled spaces, those courageous spaces, that God is able to reveal his true self to us. It is there we can experience the power of God to cover the uncoverable nakedness we, like the Emperor, are trying so desperately to hide.

Even if no one will admit it, everyone knows it: something is missing. This book is for everyone who struggles to bravely admit this reality. It's for all of us who believe that God intends more for us yet don't know how to fully step into that promise of life to the fullest.

God longs to not only clothe us with his presence but also free us from the incessant need to pretend that we have it all together. We have his open-ended promise to meet us right where we are and to impress upon us his redemption and his transforming presence. But first, we must be brave enough to tell the truth, not only to ourselves but to God. I believe that on some level, all of us are longing to do just that. We simply want reassurance that at the end of our vulnerability we will not be abandoned and exposed, stepping out only to find that we are the foolish ones.

The Scriptures hold a promise that allows us to push through our fears and find the courage within us. The promise is found in the final words of the book of Acts:

> For this people's heart has become calloused;
>> they hardly hear with their ears,
>> and they have closed their eyes.
> Otherwise they might see with their eyes,
>> hear with their ears,
>> understand with their hearts
> and turn, and I would heal them. (Acts 28:27)

Healing is our desperate need. And if we are willing to see, hear, and understand with our hearts, God will heal us.

So let us learn a life lesson from a young child. Open your eyes and say with boldness . . .

Something is missing. But transformation is possible.

2

///////////////

Something's Missing

The truth is I love being alive. And I love feeling free. So if I can't
have those things then I feel like a caged animal and I'd rather not
be in a cage. I'd rather be dead. And it's real simple. And I think it's
not that uncommon.

Angelina Jolie

I grew up being exposed to a wide variety of Christian traditions. Our
family shuttled in and out of different contexts, and I am grateful for
the view that provided me such a wide spectrum of the Christian community. It shaped in me a larger picture of God and was significant
in making me the person I am today.

There was another side benefit as well. Having the opportunity to
visit so many different kinds of churches gave me the chance to see
how common it is for Christians to feel that something is still missing.
From the outside looking in, many of these traditions seemed quite
different from each other. They had different theological emphases,
different styles of worship, and different liturgies that defined their
identity. And yet, when you got up close, it was obvious that there
was a persistent longing that bound all of them together. Something
was missing.

I saw it in my early years, growing up in conservative, fundamentalist churches. I was surrounded by people who were very serious about rightly dividing God's Word and living in light of that truth, yet I met so many who still longed for something more.

I saw it in my teen years, which were spent in charismatic, Pentecostal churches. I was surrounded by people who were very serious about encountering the living God and pursuing a Spirit-filled life, yet I met so many who still longed for something more.

I saw it during my twentysomething years, which were spent working at Willow Creek Community Church. I was surrounded by a cutting-edge, culturally relevant community committed to reaching irreligious people, yet I met so many who still longed for something more.

I saw it during my time spent working alongside Christian social activists. I was surrounded by people who took social justice, ministry to the poor, and racial reconciliation very seriously, yet I met so many who still longed for something more.

I inevitably wondered, "How can this be?" How can there be so many people who love God, have surrendered their lives to Christ, and yet still feel this persistent gap between their current spiritual reality and the fullness of God that they long for?

The search to discover what it was that was missing became a defining mark of my spiritual journey. I wanted—I *needed*—to uncover what it was that so often frustrated the collective attempts to live into the promise Jesus gave in John 10:10. My own spiritual vitality depended on it.

That quest took me down a long and winding path, and it eventually led me to a clear conclusion. I became convinced that both the source of "something's missing" and the secret to fullness of life could be found in the essence of a single word.

Faith.

Is it surprising to hear me claim that faith is the single thing missing for such a broad spectrum of Christ followers? It seemed so to me at first. After all, you can't even become a Christian without faith. So how could faith be what's missing?

The lightbulb moment for me came when I realized that I was asking the wrong question when it came to faith. I tended to think of faith as something a person either had or didn't have. But that's the wrong approach—if someone has entered into a relationship with God, they obviously possess some level of faith.

The more important question has to do with *fullness* of faith. Faith is what allows us to "be filled to the measure of all the fullness of God" (Eph. 3:19). We cannot possibly discover the fullness of life described by Jesus without correspondingly discovering what it means to have fullness of faith.

But what does fullness of faith look like? And how do we get it?

These are difficult questions to answer, because most of us have grown up in very specific traditions that capture only certain dimensions of faith. Though the particular emphasis shifts within each circle, there is a commonality that defines all of our experience. We have learned to capitalize on certain dimensions of faith that are important, yet we have also neglected other dimensions of faith that are equally integral to our ability to experience the abundant life.

This first became clear to me when I came across a very provocative definition of Christian faith:

> Faith is the perspective which enables human beings to recognize God's actions in human history. . . . The Bible makes faith something other than an ecstatic feeling in moments of silent prayer, or an acceptance of inerrant propositions. Faith is the response of the community to God's act of liberation. It means saying yes to God and no to oppressors.[1]

I read this quote as a twentysomething working at Willow Creek. Just a few months earlier I had shared with one of my mentors that I felt spiritually stagnant and was looking for ways to jump-start my walk with God. He urged me to take advantage of the restlessness I was feeling and to use that as a stimulant to pursue God in new ways.

He carried a strong conviction that one of the best ways a Christ follower grows comes when they expose themselves to voices outside of their typical stream of influences. At that point in my life, Willow Creek–type voices were my primary influence. I had learned a lot from those voices, but I was also up for the challenge to broaden my horizons.

One of the fastest growing and most influential movements in the global church was liberation theology, and he suggested I read some books from authors in that stream. (If you are unfamiliar with the term, liberation theology emphasizes the centrality of God's heart to liberate and bring freedom to his people. It starts with the exodus story of God's deliverance of the Hebrew people from slavery and follows that line all the way to the ministry of Jesus in Luke 4:18–19, when he declares that he has come to bring the same liberating power to the oppressed.)

I ended up reading a handful of books within the liberation theology movement, and I was stirred by the way they were able to integrate both sides of the "Great Commandment"—to love the Lord your God with all your heart, soul, mind, and strength, and to love your neighbor as yourself. I had memorized this as a child, but as I studied the theological reflections of these authors, I realized that I had spent far more energy in my upbringing focused on the first half than the second. Now these theologians were opening my eyes to the ways that God cares for the neighbor—particularly the neighbor that is in harm's way.

It was when I was reading the book *A Black Theology of Liberation* by Dr. James Cone that I came across the aforementioned definition of faith. Dr. Cone is arguably the most influential author to write on liberation theology from an African American perspective, and his view of faith both intrigued and unsettled me.

I was intrigued when he described faith as the perspective that enables us to "recognize God's actions in human history." Reading those words stirred something in me. It made sense that if we were connected to God by faith, we would be able to see the world as God saw it.

However, his line that faith is "saying yes to God and no to oppressors" also left me feeling unsettled. The concept itself was intriguing, but using that as a definition of faith caused me to squirm a bit. It didn't sync well with some of the other definitions of faith that I had been exposed to growing up.

But even in the squirming, I realized what a gift this was. Reading Cone's definition of faith caused me to take a step back and reflect on the different ways I had heard faith defined growing up in the church.

I went first to the dimension of faith that I recalled being most often highlighted—faith as the means to salvation. Those who emphasized this dimension of faith often pointed to verses like Ephesians 2:8: "For it is by grace you have been saved, through faith—and this is not from yourselves, it is the gift of God."

I had also heard many pastors describe faith as primarily an intellectual reality. From their perspective, faith is all about having the confidence to act on God's promises, with the assumption that you can only do that when your faith is rooted in sound doctrine and right thinking.

Other voices from my charismatic heritage would emphasize that faith was primarily about connection to the Holy Spirit. I thought of one of my former pastors who would often quote John 3. He would remind us that we serve an invisible God who operates in the spirit realm and that "flesh gives birth to flesh, but the Spirit gives birth to spirit" (John 3:6). Faith, therefore, is the divine capacity to be connected to the Spirit of God in ways that enable us to reflect and manifest that Spirit.

And then there was the justice crowd, who sounded a lot like Cone. For them, it was nearly impossible to separate the internal and external dimensions of faith. They loved the words of James, brother of Jesus:

> What good is it, my brothers and sisters, if someone claims to have faith but has no deeds? Can such faith save them? Suppose a brother or a sister is without clothes and daily food. If one of you says to them, "Go in peace; keep warm and well fed," but does nothing about their physical needs, what good is it? In the same way, faith by itself, if it is not accompanied by action, is dead. (James 2:14–17)

As I looked over this list, I was struck by how wide of a range there is when describing faith. I began to go back through each one of them and found that there wasn't a single perspective on faith that I could comfortably live without. Each one seemed integral, but each one also seemed limited and incomplete if it stood alone.

Was faith about salvation? Absolutely, but I knew faith had to be more than just a doorway into Christianity. Was faith about sound doctrine and right belief? Absolutely, but I had known people whose doctrine quotient was high but whose faith quotient was not. Was faith about connecting to the Spirit of God with clarity and power? Absolutely, but the Spirit also empowers us and sends us out with authority, so that can't be its only function. Was faith about action, as we join Jesus in the renewal of the world? Absolutely, but what a tragic omission if faith is not first being connected to God's heart and displaying an ability to discern his voice.

I began to realize just how much dimension faith has to it. On one hand, there is a beautiful simplicity to faith. Even a child can have the faith to grab on to God without having much belief or understanding, and it is still counted as an act of great faith.

On the other hand, faith has so many dimensions, and if we allow ourselves to experience only one, we lose out on the fullness of life itself. Faith is the means by which the fullness of who we are connects to the fullness of Jesus Christ. Faith is the means by which the fullness of life that we are designed for is expressed and actualized.

That's why I confidently make the claim that what's missing is faith. The question is not whether we have faith—the question is whether we have a faith that is holistic, that is multidimensional, and that ultimately leads to the fullness of life and fullness of God that we so desperately long for.

3

////////////

People of the Story

Christians are people who take their identity from someone else's story. It's not that we don't have our own story. It's that our story is part of a bigger story.

Dr. Klyne Snodgrass

What is faith? Such a simple question, and yet, in so many ways, such a complicated one. Want proof? Try googling the phrase *Christian faith* and see what a wide range of answers you get. Or try asking ten friends.

So what is faith? And how do we experience faith in such a way that it translates into fullness of life?

I grew up going to Sunday school, and it wasn't unusual for me to drift off in the middle of one of those lessons that never seemed to end. It always seemed to be right at this point that the teacher would quiz me with some random question to ensure that I was paying attention (or to point out that I wasn't). My friends and I had a running joke about times like this—it didn't matter if you were unsure of the question, you could still guarantee that the answer remained the same: "Jesus!"

So what I'm about to say next might sound just like one of those Sunday school questions. If the question is "What is faith?" what do you suppose is the right answer? "Jesus!"

Wow, what a shock, right? Jesus is the center of Christian faith. Aren't you so glad you bought this book?

How can so many people say they believe in Jesus and yet still have so many areas of their life that seem untouched by his power? Or to put it another way, how can a whole generation of Christ followers have an authentic faith connection to Jesus and yet simultaneously feel like something's missing?

One of the people who has helped me answer this question in a pointed way is Dr. Klyne Snodgrass. An accomplished author and biblical scholar, Dr. Snodgrass has spent his entire adult life studying the New Testament in particular. He thinks he knows the answer to this question.

I heard him address this question during a fantastic lecture on faith.[1] He opened the session by asking, "What is it that churches in America are missing?"

At the root of what's missing, he suggested, is an incomplete understanding of faith. He thinks we have our emphases in reverse when it comes to faith.

His primary illustration of this was how we talk about Jesus "coming into our hearts." In most Christian circles we frame the conversion process around this language. When a spiritual seeker is prepared to surrender their life to Christ, we encourage them to ask Jesus to come into their heart. This inward-focused, individualized language continues to shape the way we think about spiritual growth even as a Christian matures in their faith.

Is it bad to ask Jesus to come into your heart? Of course not. Jesus Christ is everywhere, including in our hearts. But Snodgrass's point was that the level of emphasis we place on this doesn't match the level of emphasis it receives in the Bible.

Which is a more familiar way to describe faith in Christian circles: Christ being "in us," or us being "in Christ"? Dr. Snodgrass asked his listeners to answer by raising their hands, and nearly every person in the room said that they had primarily heard faith described as Christ being *in us*. This did not surprise Dr. Snodgrass—it is what he finds to be the case everywhere he goes. The problem is that inviting Jesus into our heart is just the very tip of the iceberg.

According to Snodgrass's research, Paul uses the language of Christ *in us* five or six times in the New Testament. But when you contrast that to the frequency of us *in Christ*, you discover that this description occurs an astonishing 164 times![2]

Summarizing the importance of this distinction, Snodgrass asked, "If Christ is only in you, then how big is Christ? Not very big, and you can tuck him away when you don't need him. But," he asked, "if you and all other human beings are in Christ, as well as all of creation, then how big is Christ?" His question needed no answer—the point had been clearly made. We need a bigger and broader vision of faith. We need to learn what it means not just to invite Jesus into our life but to step into Jesus's invitation to join *his* life.

Martin Luther, the leader who ignited the Protestant Reformation with his Ninety-Five Theses in 1517, used a powerful image to make a similar point. Here is how he described holistic faith:

> But faith must be taught correctly, namely, that by it you are so cemented to Christ that He and you are one person, which cannot be separated but remains attached to Him forever and declares: "I am as Christ." And Christ, in turn, says: "I am that sinner who is attached to Me, and I to Him. For by faith we are joined together in one flesh and bone."[3]

Martin Luther says that when faith is taught correctly, we see that by faith we are *cemented* and *attached* to Christ. This is nearly identical language to the apostle Paul's emphasis of being *in Christ*.

If faith is strictly the means by which Jesus enters into my heart, it is an accurate but limited view. It leaves me feeling as if I am the one in control, with Jesus at my mercy, even if that is not what I believe on a conscious level. He goes where I go, rather than the other way around. It leaves me vulnerable to a life unchanged. The danger of this view is that I relegate Jesus to the role of spiritual add-on, and he is not unleashed to act as the spiritual force that he actually is.

If I am "in him," versus him being "in me," I am no longer in control of my life. I am anchored in Christ and to what Christ values and to what Christ says. What Jesus Christ does and where Jesus Christ goes now becomes the dominant narrative of my life. When Jesus moves, I move. When Jesus heads into uncharted waters, I go with him, even if I am filled with fear. When Jesus leads me into the unknown, I go into the unknown with him. I can't *not* go—I am cemented to him by faith.

Do you see how profound of a difference that is? If I remain in control of Jesus, then I have little hope for experiencing the fullness of life that God has designed me for. But when I see that I am cemented to Jesus, then he is the one who is in control, and he can lead me to that fullness of life—however he sees fit.

In his lecture, Dr. Snodgrass asked, "Is the idea of being 'in Christ' simple?"

He let the question hang in the air, then flatly answered, "No. It's not easy, because we haven't been taught to live like this. It's not how our pastors and teachers and theologians talk, and it's not how we talk. But it can be done—it needs to be done. We need to learn to live 'in Christ' so that we as Christians, and we as churches, can become the force of love in the world that God designed us to be!"

I agree wholeheartedly with his assessment. It can be difficult to make the transition from living from a paradigm of Christ *in me* to living from a paradigm of my life *in Christ*. It's not always clear what that means or how to do it. Yet when we hear it, something tells us that it is exactly what we need to learn.

The purpose of this book is just that—to paint a biblical picture of holistic, multidimensional faith, and to inspire and equip you to step into that as a new dimension of life in Christ. To do so, we will dive deep into Hebrews chapter 11, the most potent and expansive teaching on faith in the whole Bible.

After weaving together the story of one amazing faith hero after another, the writer of Hebrews gives us a robust vision of Christ that we need to move forward on this journey. We will lean heavily on this text throughout the rest of the book, so allow these words to saturate your heart and mind as we begin to explore the kind of faith that allows us to be "in Christ" and experience the fullness of life that God intends:

> Therefore we also, since we are surrounded by so great a cloud of witnesses, let us lay aside every weight, and the sin which so easily ensnares us, and let us run with endurance the race that is set before us, looking

unto Jesus, the author and finisher of our faith, who for the joy that
was set before Him endured the cross, despising the shame, and has
sat down at the right hand of the throne of God. (Heb. 12:1–2 NKJV)

The writer of Hebrews spends forty verses in chapter 11 sharing
the stories of men and women whose lives were utterly transformed
by faith. As faith transformed them, it in turn transformed the world
and rewrote history.

Though their stories are amazing and diverse, the writer of Hebrews
wants us to be clear that the source of power and strength remained
exactly the same for all of them. Hebrews 12:1–2 shows that it was a
comprehensive vision of Jesus Christ that allowed them to live with
this kind of faith.

The same is true for you and me. We are wise to reflect on this
vision of Jesus given to us by the writer of Hebrews. A number of
adjectives are used to describe Jesus in the New Testament, but this
is the clearest description of the nature of Jesus as it relates to our
journey of faith. Jesus works in a very specific fashion when it comes
to faith, and it is captured by the words of the writer of Hebrews. We
go on a transformational journey of faith when we "look unto Jesus,"
who is "the author and finisher of our faith, who for the joy that was
set before Him endured the cross, despising the shame, and has sat
down at the right hand of the throne of God" (Heb. 12:2 NKJV).

This incredible description of Jesus is wrapped around a pair of
colorful Greek words: *archēgos* and *teleiōtēs*. They are both unusual
words in Greek—*archēgos* is used only four times in the Bible, and
teleiōtēs is used only here.

Both of these images speak to the nature of Jesus as he leads us
into a life of dynamic faith, and because of that they become of supreme importance. The first word that the writer uses, *archēgos*, is a
particularly compelling image. Its usage in the ancient Greek world
does not clearly translate into a single English word, so commenta-
tors struggle to find the single best word. The two most common
translations of the word are *author* and *pioneer*. We need to look at
the image of *archēgos* through both the lenses of *author* and *pioneer*
to get the full meaning (*teleiōtēs* is the word translated as *finisher*).

Let's take a moment to look at the three images of Jesus given by the
writer of Hebrews: author, pioneer, and finisher of faith. Jesus loves

you, knows you, and is ready to meet you right where you are. Jesus has an incredible vision for your life, and he wants you to experience the fullness of life that you have been designed for. When you allow him to act as the *author*, *pioneer*, and *finisher* of your faith, you are not just pointed toward life—you are connected to life itself!

We Are Cemented to Jesus, the Author of Our Faith

When you enter into a great story, you also enter into an interesting relationship with the author. To participate with this great story, you first have to relinquish a great deal of control. You don't get to decide who the characters are. You don't get to decide how the plot unfolds or what the ending is going to be. You don't have control over which parts of the story are going to make you cry and which parts are going to make you laugh. You don't get to decide when the story makes your heart race and when it moves with such ease that hours go by like minutes.

Ordinarily you and I wouldn't relinquish that much control to someone. But a great story written by a great author is different. The opportunity to get swept into a story bigger than you is an opportunity too amazing to pass up. A great author will capture your imagination, touch your emotions, and transport you into another reality. A great author sweeps you into moments of transcendence. You have to surrender to the author of the story to enter into that narrative.

When we talk of cementing ourselves to Jesus as the author of our faith, we are using the language of story. We are recognizing that there is a bigger story than ours and that it is a story that is unfolding all around us. It is a narrative of a God who loves his people, but whose people have turned on God and on each other. It has a main character who loves all he created and who has a crazy plan for reclaiming that which has been lost. It is a story of restoration and of renewing, a plotline of a redeeming love, the greatest love of all.

To use the words of Dr. Snodgrass, "Christians are people who take their identity from someone else's story. It's not that we don't have our own story. It's that our story is part of a bigger story."

I have met a number of people who fear that if they surrender their life to Jesus, they will lose their individuality. They perceive themselves more like pawns in a chess game than irreplaceable characters in the greatest story ever told. They fear that if they abdicate control, they will no longer have a story, because a devoted life to Jesus will require that they leave behind their dreams and ambitions.

That couldn't be further from the truth. God's narrative doesn't swallow your narrative—it gives meaning to it. It's only as we are transposed into God's bigger story that our individual story makes any sense. It's only as you find your place in God's story that your story ends up with any meaning.

This has certainly been true for me. I grew up in a Christian home and therefore had the luxury of being exposed to biblical knowledge from early on. But my testimony is evidence that you can know the right answers but still refuse to allow Jesus to become the author of the story.

It wasn't until I made the shift—even as a professing Christian—from having myself be the author to letting Jesus being the author that I discovered true life to the full. I had no idea how my narrative was going to unfold when I made this shift. I couldn't have imagined that I would go from working at an internet start-up company to working at a suburban megachurch. I couldn't have imagined going from a suburban megachurch to spearheading an urban church plant. I couldn't have imagined that my story would require a move from a white, monocultural setting to a multiethnic, multicultural one.

And it's a good thing I couldn't imagine those things. The truth is that I would have never had the courage or foresight to respond to those huge faith moments if I had been given access to them on the front end. I have come to learn that trusting my life to Jesus as the author of faith is the most exciting way to live. There are hard moments, scary moments, and doubt-filled moments along the way. But those always give way to something even better—Jesus himself. I have learned that when I put my trust in Jesus and courageously follow him in both the small and big faith moments of life, he comes through in ways I could have never even dreamed.

I hope the same will be true for you. I hope that the vision from Hebrews of Jesus as the author of your faith will be one that reshapes the way you see and relate to Jesus. If you haven't fully made this commitment already, I hope you will now. I stand with you as we continue to make Jesus bigger in our lives, cease striving to be the author of our own stories, and allow the author of faith to take hold of the narrative from this point forward.

We Are Cemented to Jesus, the Pioneer of Our Faith

The alternative translation of *archēgos* is *pioneer*, and this brings a similar but distinct perspective to the role of Jesus when it comes to your faith. It is this translation that draws such a clear bridge for me between the Hebrews 12 picture of faith (Jesus as pioneer) and the John 10 picture of faith (Jesus as the Good Shepherd).

In John 10, Jesus describes the relationship between the Good Shepherd (himself) and his sheep (us). Martin Luther described faith as the means by which we are cemented to Jesus, and John 10 shows some of the practical ways faith binds us to the Good Shepherd. Jesus goes out before us, and we follow because we know his voice (see v. 4). We are able to distinguish between the voice of Jesus and the voice of a stranger (see v. 5). We are able to "come in and go out" from the presence of Jesus (v. 9). We are able to intimately know Jesus and be intimately known by Jesus (v. 14).

We've all heard the expression, "It's a jungle out there." Well, I actually got to *see* the jungle firsthand, and let me tell you, I now see where that expression comes from.

My wife and I took a trip to the Amazon jungle in Brazil early in our marriage. The day we arrived we met Nelson, an animated, relational local who oozed enthusiasm for life. He is one of those people who makes you tired just watching him talk. Still, his enthusiasm won us over to join him on an all-day jungle trek.

He was a trained guide for these type of trips—a "pioneer" if you will. He told us that if we would join him for this all-day hike, we would have the experience of a lifetime. We would see some of God's most beautiful and untouched creation, he promised, and we would be transported into a world full of beauty, mystery, and intrigue. It was too good of an opportunity to pass up, and we signed up on the spot.

It wasn't until the day of the hike that Nelson finally told us the other half. He had recruited a group of six brave tourists, and we were all excited and ready. But as we geared up for the starting line, Nelson suddenly got serious and gave us a little talk about the dangers that would await us on the journey ahead.

"Dangers!" shouted one of the travelers in our group. "You didn't say anything about dangers. What kind of dangers are there?" Nelson began to list them: poisonous plants, unstable cliffs, and native wildlife that was aggressive and instinctively hostile.

The excitement we'd all felt quickly began to be replaced by anxiety. Nelson looked over the faces of the group, paused, and then burst out with one of his big, trademark smiles, "What are you all so worried about? I know every inch of this rain forest. If you stay close to me, you have absolutely nothing to fear! I will lead you and I will protect you. Just stay close to me, and you will have the adventure of your life!"

We took Nelson at his word, and that was exactly what happened. He went all Indiana Jones on us and pulled out his well-worn machete to carve out a path ahead. I secretly wanted to pick up a machete and hack away with him for my own Indiana Jones moment, but I'm pretty sure I would have just made a fool of myself. I left the hard work to Nelson, and sure enough, the heavy foliage gave way, and we pushed into the unknown.

This was a living metaphor of what John 10 and Hebrews 12 describes. It gave me such a clear picture of what it means to be cemented by faith to Jesus as pioneer.

When I was younger I had a strong need for clarity. I wanted to know exactly what it meant to follow Jesus and precisely where he was taking me. I wanted to know what abilities I already possessed that equipped me for the journey, and I wanted to know which skills were currently missing so that I could begin cross-training in preparation. I wanted a map with a "You are here" sticker on it, and I wanted a GPS that showed me where I was going next.

I am still on this journey, but as I have matured in my faith, I have begun to let go of those needs and instead embrace Jesus for exactly who he says he is. Jesus never promises me clarity, or the removal of risk, or that he will spare me from an assignment that demands more than I can actually do. Clarity, confidence, and self-sufficiency allow me to feel in control, but they don't require elevated levels of faith and dependence. That is why we need a pioneer.

Jesus promises that he is the Good Shepherd and that I am the sheep. The Bible promises that Jesus is the pioneer of my faith and that he will lead me into the fullness of life that I have been designed for. But in order to get there, I have to follow him as he leads and blazes the trail.

What is expected of me is to trust him, to learn to hear his voice, and to courageously follow him when he moves. I may not be able to see the master plan or precisely where he is leading me, but I will be able to see him carving out the path right in front of me. And if I will just follow, one step at a time, he will protect and guide me into the very life that I am designed for. That is what Jesus wants to do for you as well. That is what it means to entrust your life of faith to Jesus as the pioneer.

We Are Cemented to Jesus, the Finisher of Our Faith

The final image used by the writer of Hebrews to describe Jesus is that he is the *teleiōtēs*—the *finisher* of faith. What does it mean that Jesus is the finisher of our faith?

The word that the writer of Hebrews uses is a direct reflection of the words used by Jesus on the cross. The account of the crucifixion according to the apostle John records Jesus's last words:

> Later, knowing that everything had now been finished, and so that Scripture would be fulfilled, Jesus said, "I am thirsty." A jar of wine vinegar was there, so they soaked a sponge in it, put the sponge on a stalk of the hyssop plant, and lifted it to Jesus' lips. When he had received the drink, Jesus said, "It is finished." With that, he bowed his head and gave up his spirit. (John 19:28–30)

When Jesus said, "It is finished," he used the root of the same word that would later describe Jesus as the *finisher* of our faith.

What was it that Jesus finished on the cross?

What was finished was the need to ever doubt again that you are truly loved by God. What was finished was wondering if you could really be forgiven, if you could be accepted, if you could be called a child of God. What was finished was the need to question whether you have been designed with purpose, meaning, and destiny. It was finished.

It is finished means we no longer have to work or wonder. *It is finished* means we are no longer alone in this world. *It is finished* is the end of our old selves and the beginning of a new adventure in Jesus.

The atoning work of Jesus on the cross was the highest expression of love the world has ever seen, and *it is finished* is now anything but a finish line when it comes to a life of faith. *It is finished* means we can approach the throne of grace with confidence. *It is finished* means that we can begin a new adventure of faith as we follow Jesus Christ, the author and pioneer, not into a false or domesticated version of life but into the wild—into the genuine life that we have been created for.

4

////////////

Faith in 3-D

The juice goes out of Christianity when it becomes too based on faith rather than on living like Jesus or seeing the world as Jesus saw it.

Steve Jobs

Faith is what allows us to be, in the words of the apostle Paul, "in Christ" (he says this nine times in Ephesians 1 alone!). Faith is what allows us to be, in the words of Martin Luther, "so cemented to Christ that He and you are one person."[1]

Jesus repeatedly proclaimed that he was life itself. In order to experience the fullness of life that we long for, we need to first be "in" Christ.

But as indispensable as this reality is, it can still leave us with a vague sense of how to move forward. If holistic, multidimensional faith is what's missing, then how do we find it?

This is why Hebrews 11 has become a sacred passage to me. The writer makes clear that the faith we are searching for must be rooted first in the person of Jesus. We are to "fix our eyes" on Jesus as he authors and pioneers our path of faith (Heb. 12:2).

But what does the holistic, multidimensional faith that Jesus is leading us into look like? And how do we know if we are on the right path? Are there signposts that can affirm we are heading in the right direction or caution signs that can warn us when we are not?

The writer of Hebrews uses an intriguing image to guide us into the answer to these important questions. He weaves together dozens of stories of men and women of faith throughout chapter 11, then uses this image to describe them as a collective unit: "a great cloud of witnesses" (Heb. 12:1).

What is this great "cloud of witnesses"? It is the men and women who have already gone before us as living examples of how faith in Christ can completely transform a human life. It is Abraham and Noah, Moses and David, Rahab and Sarah. It is the unnamed heroes of faith who "conquered kingdoms" and "administered justice" in the name of Jesus (Heb. 11:33). It is a thousand-year history of faith, told through a composite of amazing stories.

We often have an instinctive response to stories of great faith like this. Our insecurities flare when we contrast our seemingly ordinary life with the seemingly extraordinary lives of those captured in biblical history. Many of us feel too normal, too insecure, too commonplace, too incompetent, too sinful, too scared, and too ordinary to ever be used by God in a mighty way. We assume that the important work to be done is reserved for extraordinary leaders, seminary-trained scholars, or men and women whose level of faith greatly exceeds ours.

But does that match the description of holistic, multidimensional faith in Hebrews 11? No!

Consider the story of Joseph, who was abandoned by his brothers, was falsely accused of adultery, and then spent a huge chunk of his life in prison. Who saw an ex-inmate emerging to become the second most powerful ruler in Egypt? Or consider Rahab, who was a prostitute with no track record of spiritual heroism when God summoned her. Who could have seen her emerging to play such an important role in the Hebrew voyage to the Promised Land?

Or what about David? We know him now as a great leader and powerful king, but that wasn't how his own family viewed him. They saw him as a lowly, forgettable shepherd. When the prophet Samuel arrived in David's hometown searching for the next leader, Jesse (David's father) happily showcased his seven eldest sons as potential candidates. After meeting each of them, Samuel finally had to ask, "Are these all the sons you have?" (1 Sam. 16:11).

Jesse did have one more son, but he was too simple, too small, and too ordinary. It couldn't be David, could it? He was just a shepherd!

Jesse was certain that if Samuel was going to anoint one of his sons, the leading candidates were already sitting here before him. Samuel didn't admit it out loud, but perhaps he had the same suspicion. Could that young, ordinary shepherd boy out in the field really be the one through whom God was going to do extraordinary things? But God had spoken these words to Samuel:

> Do not consider his appearance or his height. . . . The LORD does not look at the things people look at. People look at the outward appearance, but the LORD looks at the heart. (1 Sam. 16:7)

This resembles Moses's journey into great faith as well. Insecurity plagued him every step of the way, and nobody saw him as a candidate to become such a force for good. Abandoned by his mother to save his life, Moses grew up without knowing his birth family. To compound matters, his early years were marked by high-profile mistakes, and he managed to simultaneously alienate himself from both his adopted culture (Egyptian) and his birth culture (Jewish). After killing an Egyptian, Moses was forced to flee to the wilderness. Like David, he became a shepherd. Not only did he live at the lowest level of the socioeconomic ladder, he did it for forty years!

When God revealed himself to Moses at the burning bush, the insecurity finally bubbled all the way up to the surface. Moses put words to the exact sentiment most of us feel when we come to the precipice of a new level of faith: "Who am I?" (Exod. 3:11).

I think this is the question that nips at our confidence every step of the journey toward holistic, multidimensional faith. It is so tempting to fall into this trap. We recognize something's missing, and we grow in our longing for something more. But then just as quickly, insecurity arises. We fear that great faith is not accessible to ordinary people like us, and we start to allow the vision to fade away.

The writer of Hebrews is determined to ensure that we do not fall into that trap. He insists that "Who am I?" is the wrong question and is ultimately irrelevant. The most important question when it comes to faith is not "Who am I?" but "Who is Jesus?" Great faith is not dependent on how smart, trained, or qualified you feel. Great faith is not even dependent on how great you feel about your faith. Great faith is dependent only on the source and object of our faith, Jesus Christ.

That is the truth that the writer of Hebrews wants to see penetrate to the deepest parts of your heart. The cloud of witnesses are really helpful examples of what great faith looks like, but it starts with the unbending conviction that Jesus really is the author and pioneer of faith and that he really will lead you into great faith if you will allow him to.

When you cement yourself to that Jesus, you are prepared to follow Jesus into the same type of great faith that marked the cloud of witnesses. I call this *faith in 3-D*.

What is faith in 3-D? When you enter into the stories of the great cloud of witnesses, you find that there are dimensions of faith that repeatedly resonate within the lives of those whom God calls to himself. These are the same dimensions of faith that Jesus leads us into as the author and pioneer of faith.

Faith in 3-D revolves around the following dimensions:

Dimension 1: Faith and Fear
Dimension 2: Faith and Intimacy
Dimension 3: Faith and Mission

This leads us back to the aching question: What's missing?

What is missing is a holistic, multidimensional experience of faith. What follows in the pages ahead is an unpacking of the three dimensions of faith that are essentially the missing pieces of many believing souls. Scripture admonishes us to have the audacity to truly believe Jesus wants us to experience *all three* of these dimensions of faith. They are interconnected, interdependent, and all equally important if we are to experience the fullness of life that God has designed us for.

The Prototype: Joshua

The writer of Hebrews references eighteen different individuals by name in chapter 11. He alludes to dozens more in general terms as well. It can be intimidating to try to consolidate those stories into a single, comprehensive description of faith.

Once you begin to form an understanding of holistic, multidimensional faith, though, you begin to consistently find those themes within the uniqueness of each story. Pick just about any one of the heroes of faith in Hebrews 11, and you will find all three of these dimensions as part of their faith experience.

God began a conversation with me many years ago around this idea of faith in 3-D, and one passage of Scripture that he continually drew me to for further understanding was Hebrews 11. I would read these stories and find myself asking questions like, "What prompted the writer of Hebrews to include this story in the great cloud of witnesses? What is it about this person's faith journey that demonstrated a universal principle that applies to each of us?"

Each story shaped my understanding of faith in a unique way, but the story of Joshua grabbed me in a particular way. He became a prototype for me. Wikipedia defines *prototype* as something "built to test a concept or to act as a thing to be replicated or learned from."[2]

As I studied and reflected on Joshua's story recorded in Scripture, I found it to be the primary tunnel that led me to an understanding of deeper, multidimensional faith. I was able to learn through Joshua's sacred interaction with God what it looks like to experience fullness of life as God has designed it.

We will weave in and out of the stories of many of the men and women listed in Hebrews 11 throughout the remainder of this book. We will also connect that to the journey of faith development that Jesus took his disciples through. Each step of the way, we will explore how and why these three dimensions of faith are connected and dependent on each other. And we'll see why we need to follow Jesus into all three of them if we want to experience the fullness of life.

For now, let's see how Joshua stepped into the journey God called him to. By studying the very real-life encounter (sometimes we forget that these characters of the Bible are indeed real!) between Joshua and God, we can learn to engage a similar journey of faith. The themes we watch unfold in Joshua's story are as real for us as they were for him thousands of years ago. Our journey toward faith in 3-D starts with the first dimension: faith and fear.

Dimension 1: Faith and Fear

Let's begin with the following passage of Scripture:

> After the death of Moses the servant of the LORD, the LORD said to Joshua son of Nun, Moses' aide: "Moses my servant is dead. Now

then, you and all these people, get ready to cross the Jordan River into the land I am about to give to them—to the Israelites. I will give you every place where you set your foot, as I promised Moses. Your territory will extend from the desert to Lebanon, and from the great river, the Euphrates—all the Hittite country—to the Mediterranean Sea in the west. No one will be able to stand against you all the days of your life. As I was with Moses, so I will be with you; I will never leave you nor forsake you. Be strong and courageous, because you will lead these people to inherit the land I swore to their ancestors to give them." (Josh. 1:1–6)

When Joshua describes his comprehensive faith encounter with God, he builds the platform of his story not on his eventual courage but on his immediate fear. The opening line tells us that Moses, his mentor, guide, and spiritual leader, was now dead. Moses had always been his first line of protection, but now Joshua was on his own.

I am so grateful for this authentic depiction of Joshua's interaction with God. Most leaders hide their fear and failure, choosing to trumpet their successes and victories instead. But Joshua serves us well by demonstrating an honest vulnerability about where great faith began for him—at the intersection of fear and faith.

In verse 1 Joshua points out that he had only been Moses's "aide." If Joshua listened to his fear, he would have remained paralyzed by this reality. Moses was the one who was supposed to have these huge faith moments with God, not Joshua, Moses's aide. Moses was the great leader, not Joshua, his helper.

Isn't it reassuring to remember that the great heroes of faith struggled with the same fears and insecurities that we do? I wrestle with questions like this all the time. *Can I really become a person of great faith? Can God really use someone like me to demonstrate his grace and love to the world? Is Jesus really leading me into a holistic, multidimensional faith, or am I just projecting my own desires onto him?*

What we will see over and over again is that fear and faith are closely related in the journey of spiritual transformation. Jesus will lead you out of your comfort zone and into the unknown, and you will have to rely on him at every step of the way to navigate these new realities. With each new chapter of faith come new experiences of the abundant life in Christ. But with each new chapter also come new fears. We cannot step into the life that God has designed for us without learning to first identify and master our fears.

God tells Joshua "Be strong and courageous. Do not be afraid" (v. 9). Some variation of this is repeated five times in the opening chapter. Great faith helps us to overcome great fear, but that doesn't happen by accident. We need to learn how to trust and rely on Jesus as he leads us into, and ultimately through, our fears. Faith in Jesus is what allows us to develop character defined by strength and courage.

Dimension 2: Faith and Intimacy

The words that God shares in verse 5 are precious and point directly towards spiritual intimacy with God. They speak of connectedness, friendship, and intimacy:

> As I was with Moses, so I will be with you; I will never leave you nor forsake you.

Notice that first God says, "As I was with Moses, so I will be with you." This would have been astonishing for Joshua to hear. Moses is one of only two people in the Old Testament who are referred to as a "friend" of God (Exod. 33:11; see also 2 Chron. 20:7; James 2:23). You could not have a more intimate description of intimate relationship.

The second half of the sentence affirms that which has already been made clear: "I will never leave you nor forsake you." God is inviting Joshua into an active dependence and trust in him. God knows that Joshua is scared, but he wants Joshua to move forward in faith anyway, trusting that one of the end results will be intimacy with God.

Intimacy with God is one of the central dimensions of a vital faith experience. God wants intimacy with you as well. Often God will invite you into that type of experience the same way he does Joshua. He will create an intensified faith moment where you will feel afraid, and you will have to choose between trusting in yourself and trusting in God. These moments of intensified faith create an overwhelming sense of dependency on God, and that is what leads to deep intimacy with God.

Dimension 3: Faith and Mission

Within six verses Joshua takes us into a three-dimensional faith that is alive and connected to the heart of God. Joshua's journey began at the intersection of fear and faith, then progressed into the realm of faith and spiritual intimacy with God. But as important as both of these dimensions of faith were, his journey wasn't complete until it progressed into the third realm: faith and mission.

> Be strong and courageous, because you will lead these people to inherit the land I swore to their ancestors to give them. (Josh. 1:6)

We follow a risen Savior who is alive and active in the world. He is redeeming and renewing and restoring—even at this very moment. When we connect to Jesus through faith, we are joining the redemptive movement of Jesus. We need to learn to master fear, and we need to learn to deepen our relationship along the way. But mission is what compels us to maintain a vital relationship with God.

//////////////

I love how the writer of Hebrews finishes chapter 11: "God had planned something better for us so that only together with us would [the cloud of witnesses] be made perfect" (v. 40).

That is such an incredible verse. The great cloud of witnesses represents an incredible history of faith, but that story is not yet complete. God has planned something even better for you and me! It's only as your story of faith and my story of faith are integrated into their story of faith that the ultimate story is made perfect. So don't ever let yourself think that this kind of faith is not for you or that it is somehow out of your reach! The author and pioneer of faith will lead you into this story, and your life will be forever different.

The narratives of the great cloud of witnesses become the source code for what it looks like for us to be cemented to Jesus and to experience the fullness of faith and life that we have been created for. God has planned something even better for us—let us now step into that life and into the amazing history of faith that has gone before us!

Part 2

FAITH
AND
FEAR

5

///////////////////

The Great Command

Fear and love are enemies. These two spirits will not hold the same place together. Love and fear are like light and dark . . . fresh water and salt water . . . blessing and cursing. And one of them has to win.

Danny Silk, *Building a Culture of Honor*

If someone asked you to guess the most repeated command in the Bible, what would you say?

Love people? That would certainly seem a good bet. Obey God? Seems a safe choice. Maybe something about giving money, abstaining from sex, praying more, or being active in a local church?

Though all of those are important topics addressed in the Bible, they are not associated in any way with the most repeated command in the Bible. God's most frequently repeated instruction is formulated in two simple words:

"Fear not."

Wow, would you have guessed that? I didn't.

Interestingly, the command to "fear not" is repeated in the Bible 365 times—once for every day of the year. Obviously there's something pretty significant about fear!

If we hope to encounter God in deeper ways, experience greater degrees of spiritual transformation, and step into the fullness of life that we are created for, then "fear not" becomes a mandatory addition to our vocabulary of faith.

"Fear not" was the defining reality for almost every faith hero who found their way into the "great cloud of witnesses." That includes the experience of Joshua, my prototype for faith in 3-D.

He began the account of his life at the spot of one of the most sacred encounters he ever had with God. The language was immediately grounded in fear: "After the death of Moses the servant of the LORD, the LORD said to Joshua son of Nun, Moses' aide: 'Moses my servant is dead. Now then, you and all these people, get ready to cross the Jordan River into the land I am about to give to them—to the Israelites'" (Josh. 1:1–2).

The greatest challenge that Joshua would ever face was immediately in front of him. Moses had been the spiritual mentor and guide for Joshua, but now he was dead. The Hebrews had assumed Moses would be the one to lead them into the Promised Land, but now they were filled with fear, just as Joshua was. When God invited Joshua to take the lead on this mission, I can imagine Joshua thinking, "If Moses wasn't able to get us there, how am I supposed to do it?" Whatever excitement this opportunity represented must have been dwarfed by apprehension.

What we see in the narrative of Joshua is what we see over and over again throughout Scripture: there is no such thing as moving toward great faith without first going through great fear. They live right next to each other. They are permanent neighbors in our heart.

The instinctive reply to something like this is often, "That sounds great, but we are talking about Joshua. For the people of great faith—the Abrahams, Esthers, Moseses, and Davids—that might be true. But those are special cases. I'm just an ordinary person, with ordinary faith, and with an ordinary life."

This is the story that many of us tell ourselves about great faith. It is not a true story or an accurate story, but it is a powerful story nonetheless. It goes like this: "There are certain people that God chooses to do amazing things, and then there are the rest of us. They are the ones who walk with God, have an uninterrupted line of communication, and live with near-epic levels of bravery most of the time. We can sit back and admire their great faith, but it is not something we can realistically hope to experience ourselves."

But is that really true? Should we buy into that story?

The "great cloud of witnesses" is filled with unexpected characters, which in itself should begin to poke holes in this story we so easily buy into. Hebrews 11 is decorated with outlaws and rebels, no-names and prostitutes. Wimps, cheats, adulterers, and backsliders populate the list. Is great faith really reserved for some amazing, handpicked group of people? The answer has to be no.

What about the courage necessary to step into great faith? Did the great cloud of witnesses live in some Zen-like state that transcended fear? You could never arrive at that conclusion based on an honest reading of their stories. Fear was the initial response in virtually every one of their faith journeys. "Fear not" was God's opening command to Abraham (Gen. 15:1 KJV). Fear was Moses's immediate response when God told him to deliver the Hebrews from slavery (see Exod. 3:11). Rahab referred to "great fear" in the midst of her moment of great faith (Josh. 2:9).

And then there is Joshua, who openly acknowledged the tremendous level of fear that he battled while simultaneously stepping into his moment of greatest faith. And it wasn't like Joshua was otherwise a coward—he had served as Moses's number two leader and had demonstrated his bravery in battle numerous times. But when God prepared to lead Joshua into the next chapter of great faith, great fear came right along with it.

In the New Testament Jesus has an encounter that I think may be the clearest example of fear and faith colliding. He has a conversation with a young man who was hungry, motivated, and searching for something more. Told in three different places (Matt. 19; Mark 10; and Luke 18), it is often called the story of the "the rich young ruler," though I don't particularly care for that designation, because I think it distracts from some of the important points that Jesus is trying to make about faith, fear, and fullness of life. If you immediately jump right to whatever applications Jesus is making about money in this encounter, you risk skipping over some of the best and most important stuff.

Usually when we see these intense one-on-one discussions in the Bible, they are between Jesus and someone who has an ulterior motive. In Mark 12, Jesus has a conversation with a Pharisee sent by the chief priests with the specific mission to "catch him in his words" (v. 13) by asking intentionally confusing questions. In Luke 10:25, a teacher of the law initiates a conversation with the desire to "test" Jesus. When the conversation starts to go in a different direction than he intended, he immediately works to "justify himself" (v. 29). This was something Jesus got used to dealing with—trap questions cloaked in religious language.

But this young man was different. The text presents him as someone seriously and authentically pursuing a deeper faith experience, and Jesus treats him as such. The nature of his genuine devotion is affirmed by the first part of their interaction.

Jesus says, "You know the commandments: 'You shall not commit adultery, you shall not murder, you shall not steal, you shall not give false testimony, honor your father and mother'" (Luke 18:20).

The young man replies, "All these I have kept since I was a boy" (v. 21).

With that we see that he is more than a spiritual wanderer searching for truth. He has been taught about the God of the Old Testament since he was a boy, and he has earnestly attempted to keep God's commands his whole life.

It is at that point in the conversation that the man asks what it is that's still missing. "What do I still lack?" (Matt. 19:20).

I find it interesting to see how Jesus did *not* respond. The young man was diligently focused on faithfully keeping the rules, and I therefore suspected Jesus might respond by separating legalism from grace. I expected Jesus to say something like this: "It's all about grace and God's love, not about keeping the rules and earning your way. You are too focused on the commands and too caught up on legalism, when you should instead be focused on having a relationship with God."

While that statement may be 100 percent true, it does not accurately reflect that which Jesus detected as the source of what was missing in this man's life. His problem was not legalism—it was something else.

Jesus says, "You still lack one thing" (Luke 18:22).

What an important phrase. It's just *one* thing this rich young ruler lacks. What is the one thing?

"Sell everything you have and give to the poor, and you will have treasure in heaven. Then come, follow me" (v. 22).

This is a fascinating reply, and it is filled with meaning. On one side we have an earnest, devoted man who says, "Something is missing." On the other side we have the offer of fullness of life, as Jesus concludes by inviting him to "come, follow me."

The answer that Jesus gives to *this* young man is to sell everything and give it to the poor. While Jesus often challenged people to greater levels of generosity, there is no biblical record of him telling anyone *else* to sell everything they have. Do we all need to sell our possessions and give them to the poor?

The progression of the conversation is important. Jesus begins by acknowledging the commands that are already being dutifully kept by this man. It is a list that matches well with the goals of any Christian who places a premium on personal piety and morality: sexual purity ("you shall not commit adultery"), truth-telling and honest living ("you shall not steal," "you shall not give false testimony"), and honoring the institution of the family ("honor your father and mother").

But as important as the commands regarding personal piety are (and they are!), it is interesting to note the gap between his diligence toward certain moral imperatives and his noticeably lax effort toward others—particularly toward reflecting God's heart for the poor.

This man acknowledges that he has been taught since childhood to honor the commands of the Old Testament, so it really shouldn't have been surprising that Jesus told him to give himself fully to the poor. God is consistently portrayed in the Old Testament as the one who "defends the cause of the fatherless and the widow, and loves the foreigner residing among you" (Deut. 10:18), and God drew an immediate connection between grace and concern for the poor when he said, "And you are to love those who are foreigners, for you yourselves were foreigners in Egypt" (Deut. 10:19).

There are hundreds of verses like that, and by now this young man had also heard that Jesus himself had identified with the famous messianic prophecies in Isaiah 61: "The Spirit of the Lord is on me, because he has anointed me to proclaim good news to the poor. He has sent me to proclaim freedom for the prisoners and recovery of sight for the blind, to set the oppressed free, to proclaim the year of the Lord's favor" (Luke 4:18–19).

The fact that Jesus called the young man to spend himself on behalf of the poor should not have been nearly the shock to his spiritual system that it was. That was actually part of his problem—part of his "lack." His understanding of faith was fragmented. Certain dimensions of his spiritual life were in tune with God, but others were out of sync.

This reality strikes me as relevant today. In many Christian circles there is a strict adherence to the commandments associated with personal morality but a confusing absence when it comes to the orientation of God toward the poor. Many Christians face the same problem as the rich young ruler: we have observed one list of commands but correspondingly ignored another. This imbalance is problematic.

I think of a conversation I recently had with a young man who was preparing to plant a church. He visited River City Community Church (the church I pastor) and told me how inspired he was by our commitment to justice as a tangible sign of the kingdom of God. He said that he badly wished that he could integrate this same focus into the DNA of his church plant. "Why can't you?" I asked. "You haven't even had your first service yet."

He replied, "We actually talked about it as a leadership team. But we have already decided on the mission and vision of our church, and we feel that justice and concern for the poor could potentially distract us from that core mission."

Statements like that are always confusing for me and even a little bit hard to hear. But I knew this guy had a good heart and was trying to find his way through this, so I asked a follow-up question: "What is the mission of your church?"

He replied, "We are a Great Commission church. We believe that the core call of the church is to evangelize and disciple."

I told him that he had no reason to worry—he and I were in one accord on what the mission of the church should be. I assured him that we too were a Great Commission church. This freed him up to know we were on the same page, and so I asked him another follow-up question. "If your main goal is to turn people into disciples, then how do you define discipleship?"

He thought about that for a moment and then jumped in with a list of activities and behaviors that he assumed were mandatory for a person seriously concerned about discipleship. They included the activities you might expect: read the Bible faithfully, pray, pursue sexual purity, avoid environments that might cause some form of stumbling, and so on. I remember thinking that it sounded a lot like the commandments that the rich young ruler so dutifully followed.

When he finished I told him that I too considered those to be important benchmarks for a devoted disciple. But then I asked, "Where do you talk about the role of the disciple when it comes to the poor, the sick, the hurting, and the oppressed?" He got quiet, then finally admitted that his theological worldview drew no clear connection between discipleship and serving the poor.

So I gave him a challenge. I said, "Go back and read the four Gospel accounts through the lens of discipleship and ministry with the poor. Decide for yourself—is this some peripheral activity that I am overemphasizing? Or is it the opposite, as I believe—a core focus of discipleship that somehow many of us have learned to neglect?"

He took me up on the challenge, and he was in a completely different frame of mind when we next met. His opening words reflected that, and were so refreshing. "Wow, I never realized how dominant the theme of serving with the poor was in the life of Jesus. When you read it from that angle, it almost seems like it was the primary thing that he and the disciples did. How have I never noticed this before? I will never talk about discipleship again without including this important dimension!"

I was thrilled for this young man and for the church he was about to start. I was confident that this broader, more comprehensive view of Christian discipleship would pay immediate dividends for him and the church community.

I believe that this is a big part of what Jesus was saying to the rich young ruler, and what he would say to us if we asked the same type of question. Jesus was helping this young man realize that one of the reasons he was experiencing a lack of spiritual vitality was because he had a fragmented, imbalanced view of faith.

The good news was that the solution to that problem lay directly in front of him. What transpired next was a clearer outcome than this young man could have possibly dreamed of: "Jesus looked at him and loved him. 'One thing you lack,' he said. 'Go, sell everything you have and give to the poor, and you will have treasure in heaven. Then come, follow me'" (Mark 10:21).

The opening of that verse is key—Jesus was motivated by love. This encounter was not fundamentally about a confrontation; it was an invitation. Jesus looked at him, loved him, and decided to extend an invitation to the most incredible opportunity that this young man could imagine: *Come, follow me.*

Many of us have heard that phrase a lot, especially if we grew up around Christianity, and it has lost some of its luster. When we read about Jesus saying something like that, we can easily miss how unusual and provocative it actually was.

That phrase—*come, follow me*—had tremendous history and significance. It was a phrase used by a rabbi, and it was used very sparingly. When a young man heard these words from a rabbi, it was like a college applicant hearing that they got accepted to Harvard or someone finding out that they just won the lottery.

The word *rabbi* comes from the Hebrew word that translates as "great one" or "master," and it was among the most prestigious positions in first-century Jewish society. To be called "Rabbi" was more than just an honor—it was the dream of every young boy (unfortunately, in a patriarchal society, girls weren't allowed to dream like this). Clergy are not thought of very highly in today's culture, but that is a direct contrast to the world of Jesus. When you asked a young Jewish boy what he wanted to be when he grew up, there was never any hesitation: "I dream of being a rabbi."

Another big contrast between someone who is a clergyperson in our modern culture and someone who was a rabbi back then is that in today's culture, if you gain the proper credentials, you can choose to pursue the pastorate as a vocational option. But you didn't get to choose back then—all you could do was enroll in a hypercompetitive process with the hope that some day a rabbi would choose *you*.

The process began with *bet sefer*, and boys aged five to ten would begin their training here. Every Jewish boy was expected to memorize the entire Torah (Genesis, Exodus, Leviticus, Numbers, and Deuteronomy), and if you didn't have it entirely memorized by age ten, you were no longer eligible for consideration.

The process continued with *bet talmud*, and boys aged ten to fourteen were expected to memorize the remainder of the Old Testament. Once these students demonstrated their ability to memorize the whole Hebrew Bible, rabbis would begin to quiz them. The rabbis required a demonstrated ability to not just memorize but also to interact with the text, to give insightful commentary on it, and to engage in spirited question-and-answer sessions. If the preteen passed all of those tests, he would then be considered a legitimate prospect.

But even the status of "legitimate prospect" took you only so far. A rabbi would never actually invite a prospect to be his *talmudeen* (what we might call his apprentice or protégé). It was considered beneath a rabbi to recruit or pursue anyone. So the pressure was completely on the prospect to approach the rabbi whom he looked up to. When he did, he would usually say something like, "Rabbi, I want to become your disciple, your talmudeen, your student. Please let me in your house of study."

This was a brave and risky thing to do, because only a small percentage was accepted. The expected path, even for the brightest prospects, was to be denied and sent instead to join the vocation of their father.

But there was the rare case where the rabbi would accept the prospect. That acceptance would come in the form of a single phrase: *Lech Acharai.*

Which in English translates as, "Come, follow me."

To actually hear those words—there was nothing like it. It was like a young kid dreaming all of their life of hitting the game-winning shot in the NBA Finals . . . and then it actually happens! That was what it felt like to hear the phrase *Lech Acharai.*

Once I came to understand that process, it shed an entirely new light on why the twelve disciples immediately responded to Jesus as they did. When Jesus walked up, for instance, to the two sons with their father and said, "Follow me" (see Matt. 4:18–20), do you now understand why they responded without hesitation?

Jesus was a real rabbi. We think of him as Savior, Son of God, and King, but he was also a rabbi. To be invited to follow him was more than an incredible honor—it was a game-changing invitation that required no reflection. They had dreamed of this as boys but assumed the opportunity to be a *talmudeen* had already come and gone. When a real rabbi came and said, "Come, follow me," they didn't need their father's permission. They knew he was already glowing with pride.

That is what is so beautiful about this encounter between Jesus and the rich young ruler. The young man feels a lack in his spiritual vitality and pursues Jesus for wisdom as to the source of what is missing. Jesus takes him seriously, responds directly to the question, and then extends an invitation that was absolutely unbelievable: "Come, follow me. Enter into an ongoing relationship with me, and be forever changed."

If fullness of life was what this young man was on the search for, then could this conversation have possibly gone any better? The Son of God himself was inviting him into relationship. He was inviting the young man to "drop the nets" of his wealth and to join up with Jesus and the disciples.

And yet, amazingly, the young man was unable to accept the invitation. Though his faith was real, his fear was greater.

This is where we can all learn so much from the rich young ruler. Our faith is real, but so is the fear of losing something we possess. What Jesus was pointing out to this young seeker, and what he is lovingly trying to point out to us, is that what we think we own was never ours to begin with.

Many of us are in the same place as this man who was so close to having it all but had to give it all first. For him, for me, for us, the fear of losing what we cherish most must loosen its hold on our hearts before we can surrender to the One who is offering us the fullness of life.

This is no easy battle to win, but like the great heroes of faith before us, we know we have the one thing we need to overcome even the greatest fear: the One who whispers into our frightened hearts, "Fear not. I am with you."

6

Boundary Breaking

Genuine self-acceptance is not derived from the power of positive
thinking, mind games, or pop psychology. It is an act of faith in the
grace of God alone.

Brennan Manning, *Ragamuffin Gospel*

I have come to deeply appreciate the encounter between Jesus and
the rich young ruler, for it illustrates the single most important thing
I have learned about the relationship between fear, faith, and fullness
of life: *fear sets the limits of life; faith expands the boundaries of life.*

That is why it is so important to acknowledge the presence of fear
and its potential impact. It is why "fear not" is the most repeated
command in the Bible. Fear sets the limits of life, both in big ways
and in small ways. Consider some everyday examples:

- If you are afraid of flying, that fear sets limits as to how you
  can get from one place to another.
- If you are afraid of heights, that fear sets the limits for how
  high you go.
- If you are claustrophobic, that fear will keep you away from any
  place that appears enclosed.

- If you are afraid of strangers, that fear will keep you from meeting new people.

Those fears might seem inconsequential, especially when talking about something as grandiose as fullness of life. But the limiting nature of fear doesn't stop there. It spreads into every important arena of life when unchecked. Consider, for instance, some of the ways fear sets limits in our relationships:

- If you are afraid of conflict, that fear will dictate the depth of your relationships. You will lose the ability to either give or receive constructive criticism, something we all badly need.
- If you are afraid of rejection, that fear will limit your ability to be truly authentic. You will find yourself choosing safety over risk in relationships, or you will choose not to move toward certain people because of your fear of rejection.
- If you are afraid of intimacy, that fear sets the limit for how vulnerable you are capable of being. You will find yourself hiding important things about yourself and failing to explore important arenas of the lives of those you love.

Consider some of the ways fear sets limits on our ability to grow spiritually, and therefore in faith:

- If you are afraid of admitting that you are wrong, you are limited in your ability to confess your sins and experience the forgiveness of God.
- If you are afraid that you have sinned too greatly, you are limited in your ability to receive the grace and freedom that comes from God.
- If you are afraid of admitting that you are broken, you are limited in how much you can experience healing through Jesus.
- If you are afraid of giving up control, you are limited in how much Jesus can lead you into the mission of God that you have been created to participate in.
- If you are afraid that your life has little purpose or meaning, you will be limited in how much you can put your trust in Jesus to lead you into the life that you were designed for.

- If you are afraid of giving up something that is toxic to your life but that you have come to depend on, you cannot experience the freedom from the thing that enslaves you.
- If you are afraid of looking foolish by believing in a God that you cannot prove or see, you will be trapped in a life of spiritual emptiness rather than living a life of vibrant fullness.

It's one thing to say you are afraid of heights. Perhaps the fear of high places doesn't seem like a life-defining reality. But when fear prevents you from engaging in authentic community or from responding to risky invitations from God, you begin to realize how powerful fear can become, and therefore how dangerous.

Nobody wishes for his or her life to feel boxed in. Nobody wants the potential of his or her life to be unnecessarily constricted. And I've never met a Christ follower who wants to intentionally prohibit Jesus from leading them toward fullness of life.

But that is exactly what happens when we allow fear to have free reign. Fear sets the limits of our life, and if we do not allow Jesus to lead us through that fear, we will remain stuck and stagnant.

Those who know me as an adult describe me as extroverted, secure, and high-energy, but that couldn't be more opposite from how I would have been described growing up. Words like depressed, isolated, and withdrawn come much closer to the actual description of me through high school.

Fear was a constant companion growing up. It began with a transient childhood, fueled by a messy divorce and numerous custody battles. Over a seven-year stretch, I was in a different school every year.

As the new kid, my greatest desire was to find a group of friends to fit in with. But the presence of fear was powerful, and I rarely found the internal fortitude necessary to take a relational risk. The result was devastating, and the limits that began to be placed on my life were significant. I was alone and isolated at each school. I never went to a single school social event during high school—not a dance, prom, or a rally. I just shrunk into my own private corner of the world and essentially gave up.

Fear's desire to grab hold of more real estate in my life wasn't just limited to making new friends. Another desire of mine was to be academically successful, go off to a good college, and eventually enter the workforce as a well-educated and equipped adult. Unfortunately, in the schools I went to, the academically oriented kids were considered nerds. My fear of rejection was so high that I intentionally sabotaged my grades just enough to ensure that I wasn't perceived to be part of the nerd circle. It was one more self-inflicted limitation. (I wish I knew then what I know now—that nerds are the ones running the world.)

I also longed to harness and develop any athletic ability I had, but this was suffocated by fear as well. I would attend school sporting events and fantasize about what it would be like to be one of the contributing members of the team. The desire was strong enough that I almost tried out a handful of times. But each time I prepared to take a risk, fear would reclaim its ascendancy. I would think, "What if I try out for the team and find out that I have absolutely no skills?" That had the potential to turn into a public spectacle, and I wasn't prepared to overcome the embarrassment. Once again, fear had set the limits of my life.

That is why I am so drawn to the encounter between Jesus and the rich young ruler. It shows how closely fear and faith live next to each other in the human heart.

I think the young man genuinely possessed faith. He was sensitive to the commands of God, and he was drawn toward Jesus. He knew he was still lacking something, and he asked Jesus to help him discern what was missing.

But he was also filled with fear. While his self-assessment pointed to full devotion to God, it did not include an accurate perception of the degree to which fear was placing limitations on him. He thought he was free and following God, but just under the surface lived a subtle but powerful set of fears that were holding him captive.

Along came Jesus, and we get to see what a great shepherd does when one of his loved ones is trapped. Jesus is in the freedom business, not the boundary business, so he employed the same shepherding strategy with this young man that he uses for us. He brought him directly to the intersection of faith and fear.

A whole new dimension of faith was opened up to the young man with these words: "Come, follow me" (Luke 18:22).

But a whole new dimension of fear was also revealed with these words: "Sell everything you have and give to the poor" (Luke 18:22).

Why was that statement so terrifying for this young man? I'm guessing that at a certain level any one of us would feel anxiety if we heard this command. But the account suggests that he had an abnormally intense reaction. The moment he heard what Jesus was asking of him, he dropped his head and was filled with sadness.

For some reason, the prospect of having to pry his fingers off of the deep affection he felt for money was evoking a fundamental fear. His identity was all wrapped up with his wealth. And the prospect of being separated from that wealth unleashed tremendous fear and anxiety.

That is the thing about fear. Whatever we fear, we are ultimately subject to. I think this young man really loved God and genuinely wanted to be obedient. But he also loved money, and the direction of his life was dictated as much or more by that love as it was by God.

Once Jesus brought him to the brink of his fear, the truth came out. His identity was cemented to what money could provide, and even the offer to experience the abundant life in Christ was unable to pry him free from its grip.

Gary Haugen, the founder of International Justice Mission, has written a lot of great stuff on fear and faith, and one of my favorite quotes is this: "For many of us the boundary of our range of action is determined by our ultimate fears . . . and our fears often remain hidden (even from ourselves) right up to the very moment when we must act."[1]

That is exactly what was happening in this encounter. The boundary of this young man's range of action was determined by his ultimate fear, which in this case was the fear of losing his wealth (and the lifestyle and identity that came with it). Fear was setting the limits of his life and ultimately holding him hostage. Jesus loved him and was trying to help him break free of the boundaries that fear was placing onto him.

Are you able to recognize this dynamic interplay between fear and faith in your life? As you look over the story of your life, do you see the ways that Jesus has brought you to the intersection of fear and faith?

This is one of the primary ways that Jesus shows his love for us. It doesn't usually feel warm and fuzzy in the moment, but Haugen is right. The boundary of our range of action is determined by our ultimate fears, and those fears often remain hidden until Jesus creates an environment or stimulus to bring them to the light. The particular boundary or limit created by fear is different for each of us, as is the circumstance by which that fear is revealed.

I think of a couple with whom I did marital counseling. They were having conflict in a couple of different areas and asked if I would help them sort through the tangled threads.

The most immediate and pressing conflict had to do with money, which did not come as a huge surprise. Money is one of the most common sources of stress in a marriage, and I often meet with couples as they try to navigate this tricky terrain. What exacerbated the struggle for this particular couple, though, was the heavily spiritual language that saturated the conflict.

The wife had grown up the daughter of a missionary, and she saw how much money could do and how far it could go to help people, and her upbringing had really shaped a spirit of generosity in her. As a result, she was able to give away huge chunks of money with ease, and she felt like this was part of her God-given identity.

This spirit of generosity had the reverse effect on her husband. He had grown up very differently than her and with a very different set of values. His family had stressed the importance of financial security and therefore strongly advocated an aggressive approach to savings and retirement planning. The ease with which his wife was able to give away money exposed some of his deepest fears around money. He didn't like being thought of as the one that was ungenerous or miserly. He also considered his approach to be the more rational and responsible perspective, and he wished she would respect that more.

They were also really struggling with the concept of intimacy, and it was quickly becoming a sore spot. I admit that when I first heard this, I gave in to my stereotypes and assumed that the wife was the one who wanted more intimacy and that the husband was resisting. But I was wrong. He had grown up in a very relational family atmosphere that stressed authenticity and vulnerability, and it had set him up well for marriage. It is common for me to do premarital counseling with men who struggle with the concept of emotional intimacy, but that was not the case with him. His parents had done a great job of nurturing this ability within him, and he was the one pursuing deeper levels of emotional intimacy within the marriage.

But each time he would pursue deeper degrees of emotional intimacy with his wife, she would withdraw. He was confused and hurt by this, and he was struggling to understand the problem. What we eventually discovered was that she had carried a number of wounds into marriage from previous relational damage, and she had developed a deep fear of emotional intimacy in response. Though the husband found it quite easy to reveal his full emotions to her, she was unable to do the same. And the more he exposed himself to her in vulnerable ways, the more her own fears around safety would get triggered.

As we continued to discuss and explore, something became clear to all three of us. Though the specific dynamics of each of their struggles appeared quite different on the surface, they were having a nearly identical struggle. Marriage had brought each of them into contact with their deepest, most fundamental fears. The husband had a fundamental fear around security, and the generosity she so easily expressed was continually flaring that fear. The wife had a fundamental fear around trust, and the husband's pursuit of emotional intimacy was continually flaring that fear for her.

Counseling this couple was a formative experience for me, because it demonstrated how prevalent fear is in every arena of life. It wasn't just my upbringing that had been affected by fear—fear impacts each one of us in significant and unique ways. Fear is a powerful and pervasive reality, and when left unaddressed, it places significant boundaries on our lives.

What makes fear dangerous—particularly our fundamental fears— is its hidden nature. If you had interviewed this couple I was counseling before they got married and asked if they were controlled by fear, they would have confidently answered no! And yet that wasn't the full truth. Fear was at work in their lives, subtly creating boundaries and limitations on how far they could go in life.

For the husband, significant boundaries were already forming around his ability to be generous. He didn't have the self-knowledge yet, but his fears around issues of security and control went deep. A constant "what-if" game would play in his head, and he would picture every bad thing that could potentially happen. The only thing that calmed him, so he thought, was to stash away large amounts of savings. He later admitted that if these fears had not been identified, he almost certainly would have lost any ability to be generous.

For the wife, significant boundaries were already forming around her ability to be emotionally intimate with another person. She didn't have the self-knowledge yet, but her fears around trust went deep. She later admitted that if the fears had not been identified, she would have learned to settle for superficial relationships across the board. She had already been actively establishing intimacy boundaries with her "close" friends, and this would have been just the beginning had she not been set free from her fears.

Fear does the same thing to us as it did to them: it draws boundaries and sets limits on our life. It's what fear did to the rich young ruler. It's what fear will do to us if we fail to acknowledge its presence and learn how to follow Jesus out of our fears and into a faith-filled life.

As the Good Shepherd, and as the author and pioneer of our faith, Jesus brings us directly to the boundary of our fundamental fears. The context for this can take so many different shapes. For the couple I was counseling, marital conflict was the catalyst. Sometimes a new opportunity is the catalyst, and other times it is a crisis. At times it is a conversation with a friend, and other times it happens during a time of self-reflection and prayer.

When Jesus does bring us to the boundary of our great fears, the most natural temptation is to run. Nobody likes to admit they are afraid, much less stare their greatest fear in the eye.

But if we can understand the "why" behind Jesus taking us toward our fear, we can begin to develop a more courageous outlook on facing fear. We realize that Jesus loves us and that he refuses to allow us to be restricted by fear. He is trying to lead us into fullness of life, and he can't get us there without breaking us free from those fears.

That is what Jesus did for the couple I had been counseling. They decided that they could view their fear as either a threat or a gift. If they viewed it as a threat, the temptation would be to justify their behaviors and vilify their partner. But if they chose to view it as a gift, they could trust that God had brought them together to help set them on a new journey toward freedom.

They chose to view it as a gift and leaned hard into the loving guidance of Jesus in their lives. After finishing our round of marital sessions, they decided to each do a series of one-on-one sessions with a Christian counselor to explore the roots of some of those fears. There they began to discover that much of what was being triggered in their new marriage relationship was directly tied to formative experiences from their upbringing. They found that even many of the good things that they learned from their families of origin ended up reinforcing some of their fundamental fears.

Armed with a new sense of emotional awareness and health, they then turned to their community group at the church for ongoing support. They mutually decided to share in detail the journey they had been on with the group of friends they were closest to. They asked this group of friends to walk with them in support and accountability as they learned to relate to each other in healthier ways.

The end result was nothing short of life changing. Those who knew them well marveled at the ways in which their fear-induced limitations began to melt away. The husband found ways to merge responsibility and generosity that were amazing to watch. The wife found ways to slowly open herself up to her husband, and the intimacy she developed there began to spread into relationships with family and friends as well. They became one of the most beloved couples in our community, and to this day they are still a go-to family for those seeking life wisdom and advice.

This couple discovered the same thing that I have found to be true time and again in my own life: fear sets the limits of life, but faith expands the boundaries. When I allow great fear to have the final word (whether knowingly or unknowingly), my life is restricted, and I become a lesser version of myself. But when I allow Jesus to lead me by faith through those fears, I become a better and fuller version of myself.

I love the way Brennan Manning describes this journey to inner wholeness: "Genuine self-acceptance is not derived from the power of positive thinking, mind games, or pop psychology. It is an act of faith in the grace of God alone."[2]

Ultimately I cannot make fear go away with positive thinking, mind games, or pop psychology. Only faith in the One who knows me and knows the path toward fullness can take me to the place of freedom I so desperately long for.

That is also why I love the sacred words that God shared with Joshua. It is exactly what I feel like Jesus is saying to me each time he brings me to a new manifestation of the intersection of faith and fear:

> Have I not commanded you? Be strong and courageous. Do not be afraid; do not be discouraged, for the LORD your God will be with you wherever you go. (Josh. 1:9)

God knew Joshua's particular boundary of fear and invited him to cross it. If Joshua had chosen fear, he would have chosen a life with restrictions and boundaries. But to choose faith was to choose a life that crossed over those fear-induced boundaries. It was a life of walking with God, a life of adventure and intimacy, mystery and excitement.

When the writer of Hebrews tells us to fix our eyes on Jesus, the author and pioneer of faith, he is inviting us to live in the exact same way.

7

///////////////

Sink or Swim

God never calls us to do something we can do in our own strength.
He always calls us to get in over our heads—to move out to where
we'll have to either depend on His power or sink.

Dr. John Perkins

Shortly after finishing the most potent section on faith in the entire
Bible, the writer of Hebrews says this:

> Remember your leaders. . . . Consider the outcome of their way of life
> and imitate their faith. Jesus Christ is the same yesterday and today
> and forever. (Heb. 13:7–8)

Great faith comes only from cementing ourselves to Jesus Christ,
who is the same yesterday and today and forever. Yet the same writer
who emphasizes this reality also tells us that we can gain a significant
boost by learning from faith leaders that have gone before us. There
is something about stepping into their stories that helps us flesh out
faith in a way that makes following Jesus a little bit more concrete.

I will never forget the first time I spent a week with Dr. John Perkins, founder of the Christian Community Development Association,
in his hometown of Jackson, Mississippi. I had never seen a city so

71

impacted by the life of one person. As we toured the town, I saw health clinics and youth centers started by him and his ministry. I walked in and out of dozens of homes that had been built by his ministry in partnership with families that were once mired in poverty and now owned their own place. I saw gardens and playgrounds his ministry had built, now brimming with joyful children.

While with Dr. Perkins, I realized it was spiritual transformation that fueled everything. He was more than just some humanitarian hero—this was a man who walked closely with God.

On my second trip to Jackson, I was able to join Dr. Perkins for an extended tour of his hometown. During our all-day trip, we saw both the beauty of his ministry and the pain that had forged the man he had become. As we saw the places and heard the stories of some of the things that had happened to him, we realized just how much Dr. Perkins had been through. Fear had been part of every stage of the journey for him, and it was faith alone that had carried him through.

His story began in 1930, when he was born into a two-bedroom house located on a cotton plantation near the small town of New Hebron, Mississippi. He came of age in one of the most violent and racist eras in our country's history. While growing up he was mocked and cursed on a daily basis and was regularly shot at with BB guns by kids in the neighborhood. Though his rage hungered for an outlet, he was warned that retaliation could literally get him killed. Powerless, he had no choice but to accept that fear and anger were unavoidable realities.

Shortly after World War II, his hero, role model, and older brother, Clyde, returned from the war. Unfortunately for Clyde, being a decorated war hero didn't improve his standing back home in the white community. The mayor of his hometown had always been wary of Clyde, and his triumphal return now made the mayor even more nervous. Fear, ignorance, and hatred came to a head one horrible night in 1946.

On that Saturday night Clyde was waiting in the Jim Crow line at the Carolyn Theater. He and some other men were horsing around, showing off for their girlfriends. The sheriff (who had been directly appointed by the mayor) was standing nearby and warned them to be quiet. Clyde playfully tried to engage him in conversation, but the sheriff instead clubbed Clyde with his baton. Clyde grabbed the club instinctively out of self-defense, and that was all the provocation the sheriff needed. He stepped back and shot Clyde twice in the stomach. Clyde would die in the lap of sixteen-year-old John Perkins that night.

Years later, in 1970, John Perkins and his wife, Vera Mae, had established an incredible ministry in Mendenhall, Mississippi, called Voice of Calvary (VOC). VOC was focused on comprehensive community transformation and development and would eventually become one of the core models that served as the origins for the Christian Community Development Association (CCDA).

VOC had been formed at the height of the civil rights movement, and Mendenhall had become one of the epicenters of civil rights activity. Tensions were high between the black and white communities, and Dr. Perkins had become one of the targets of the local authorities. His consistent work and organizing on behalf of the poor was seen as an unwelcome intrusion.

Fear of both the outlaws and the authorities were now everyday realities for the Perkins family. Their home had been victimized numerous times by Ku Klux Klan drive-bys. They had received multiple death threats. Out of concern for the family's safety, the Perkins's home was put under twenty-four-hour, seven-days-a-week security.

Things came to a violent head on February 8, 1970, when a trap was set for Dr. Perkins. Two vanloads of black college students, chauffeured by two white VOC volunteers, left Mendenhall after a day of protest and picketing on the main street and town square. As soon as the vans crossed into the next county, the police pulled them over and ordered everyone out. The black students were lined up and patted down while the white driver, Doug Huemmer, a VOC volunteer, was singled out for special punishment and cruelly beaten.

The other driver, Louise Fox, saw what happened from a distance. She rushed to a phone to call Dr. Perkins. What she didn't know was that this was all part of the sheriff's plan. The sheriff was looking for a way to arrest Perkins so that he could hand him over to the lawless guards in the prison.

When Perkins got the news, he and two other men immediately left for the Rankin County justice complex. When they arrived, they were surrounded by twelve patrolmen who searched them, then hustled them inside the building. That's when Perkins realized he'd been set up.

What followed Dr. Perkins called the longest night of his life. The racial taunts and body blows turned into nonstop beatings. For two straight hours, in a musty room with cement walls and a bare floor, Perkins and his friend Curry Brown were beaten and tortured. When it was over, the students tending to his wounds were certain he'd be dead by morning.

This is the point where the story becomes absolutely amazing to me. Perkins so badly wanted to give in to fear, anger, and hatred. He was certain that if he lived through this night, he would have to retaliate. And yet, despite being bruised and battered, Perkins sensed the presence of God come upon him, calling him to move instead toward healing and forgiveness.

He heard God whisper a single phrase: *"Love was the final battle."* He sensed God telling him that he would survive this night and that he was being summoned to step into a whole new realm of reconciliation. Love was the final battle, and he was going to preach that love to blacks, to whites, and to people of every tribe and tongue.

The effect of this visitation from God took effect immediately. The fear and anger began to vanish, and Perkins looked directly into the eyes of those who were torturing him. He could now see beyond their hatred and bitterness, and he saw that it was actually they who were dominated by fear, not him. They had been taught to hate themselves and to hate black people, but they had no idea why. Blind fear was fueling their actions.

What Perkins saw through his broken vision was people who were lost, confused, and broken. He could see firsthand what the hatred of racism did to the human heart. He was certain in that moment that the love of Jesus was what they needed.

Love was the final battle.

///////////

Dr. Perkins knows the reality of fear and faith to a level that goes beyond that of most people. So when he speaks on this topic, I am quick to listen.

I once asked Dr. Perkins what passage had most influenced his understanding of faith and fear. Without hesitation he took me to Matthew 14, where Jesus walks on the water. "That passage is all about fear and faith," he told me, and he was absolutely right. He wrote extensively about this encounter in his book *With Justice for All*:

> God never calls us to do something we can do in our own strength. He always calls us to get in over our heads—to move out to where we'll have to either depend on His power or sink. . . . Ever since God first called me, I have lived on the verge of panic. I've always been in over my head. I've always been doing things I knew I couldn't do. I've been like Peter walking on the water—always on the verge of sinking because he was doing something that took more power than he had. If he took his eyes off of Jesus—off of God's power—and looked at the storm, he would sink.[1]

God never calls us to do something we can do in our own strength. Faith is not about some blind leap into the unknown, and it's so much more than just keeping the rules. It's about cementing ourselves to Jesus and depending absolutely on his power and provision as he leads us into waters that are over our head.

Great faith will inevitably leave us feeling like we are on the verge of sinking, because we are living a life that requires more power than we possess in our natural strength. And yet, when we keep our eyes locked on Jesus, the author and pioneer of our faith, we can experience things and go places that we never could have otherwise.

//////////

Let's take a closer look at the Jesus walking on water story found in Matthew 14:22–36. The disciples had just seen Jesus perform the spectacular miracle of turning a couple of loaves and fish into a meal for a few thousand people. Now Jesus senses it is an opportune time to once again bring his disciples to the intersection of fear and faith.

The disciples get on a boat to cross the sea, and Jesus tells them he'll catch up with them a bit later. This was not unusual, as he often broke from the group for extended times of solitude, prayer, and reflection.

Just before dawn he sensed the time was right. Jesus could have waited until the disciples docked on the other side of the sea. Instead, Jesus walked out to them, *on the water*.

The disciples saw him from a distance and were filled with fear. Wouldn't you be if you saw someone walking on the water? Trying to make sense of it, one of them said, "It's a ghost" (v. 25).

Soon Jesus was close enough to the boat that they realized it was him, yet they remained confused and afraid. His first words to them included the most repeated command in the Bible: "Take courage. It is I. Do not be afraid" (see v. 27).

What gives? He created an intentional moment of fear, knew they would be afraid, but then told them not to be afraid. What was Jesus up to?

If "Do not be afraid" was said in isolation, it might be confusing. But it wasn't—Jesus added on to that. "Take courage. It is I" (v. 27). (Sounds almost identical to what God said to Joshua, doesn't it?)

Jesus wasn't saying it was bad or wrong to be afraid. He knew that would be their instinctive response. Instead, what he tells them is to not *stay* afraid. By walking on the water, Jesus was creating for them a supernatural vision of himself that gave them the capacity to overcome any of the limitations that fear was thrusting upon them.

This is so helpful for me to remember. I am afraid a lot, and if it were a sin to be afraid, then I am certain I would be in a near constant state of sin. But the problem is not that we feel afraid. The problem comes when we are afraid and stay that way. The problem comes when fear is allowed to become the dominant narrative of our life. When fear overshadows faith, our world becomes smaller. Fear causes us to retreat and seek self-protection. It stifles our ability to respond to Jesus when he shows up in daring and unexpected places of our lives.

Faith, on the other hand, expands the boundaries of what we are able to experience. Faith is what allows us to follow Jesus into the fullness of life. Dr. Perkins says that his life reflects a pattern of faith and fear that calls him to either depend on God's power or to sink. There is no in-between. The same dynamic will happen as Jesus leads you into deeper faith. You will often have thoughts like this:

I don't know if I can really pull this off.

I don't know if I am really up for this challenge.

I don't know if I have what it takes to step into this endeavor that God has designed for me.

We will battle great fear along the way, but the upside of abundant faith is so much greater. When we keep our eyes on Jesus, the author and pioneer of our faith, we are able to accomplish things we could never do in our own strength. This is the point when you are most fully alive: when you are not sure if you can actually live the life God has called you to, but you become absolutely certain that you can't live for anything less.

We are going to have to make a fundamental choice: Do we want to be safe, or do we want to be brave?

8

//////////////

Safe or Brave

One isn't necessarily born with courage, but one is born with potential. Without courage, we cannot practice any other virtue with consistency. We can't be kind, true, merciful, generous, or honest.

Maya Angelou

Whenever I share a story like that of Dr. Perkins, I do so with a degree of hesitation. On one hand, I love stories like his, and I think that the writer of Hebrews is right when he encourages us to remember our leaders. We can learn so much from their way of life, and it's encouraging that the Bible actually prods us to imitate their faith.

On the other hand, I worry that stories of great faith can inadvertently trigger another one of the many forms of latent fears that plague each of us: the fear that great faith is reserved for only a select few men and women. We are tempted to respond to every fresh move of God with the same old question of insecurity: *Who am I?*

We feel too normal, too insecure, too commonplace, too incompetent, too sinful, too scared, and too ordinary to ever be used by God in a mighty way. We assume that if there is important work to be done, it is reserved for extraordinary leaders, seminary-trained scholars, or men and women whose level of faith greatly exceeds ours.

But to give in to that insecurity is to miss the entire point of what their stories are pointing toward.

Maya Angelou says courage is not something we just enter the world with; instead, it's something we enter the world with the *potential* for. That's a big difference. Courage is like most virtues—you don't accidentally become a person of nobility, generosity, or kindness. Those are reflections of your character, and your character is a reflection of conscious choices that you make over and over again.

Have you ever heard someone say, or said yourself, "That person is so strong! I wish I could have that kind of strength"? The truth is, the person we envy isn't some kind of genetically blessed superhero. They are working with the exact same raw material as you and I. They are simply making different choices with their lives, and those choices add up over time to something that looks like the in-depth character we perceive from the outside.

The same is true of courage. Courage is not a genetic trait you inherit. Courage is a reflection of your character, and courageous fortitude comes only through a set of conscious choices that are made over and over again.

That's what makes the encounter in Matthew 14 so important. Jesus is trying to strengthen and deepen the internal character of his disciples, and specifically, he is trying to instill the virtue of courage. Courage isn't learned in a vacuum, though—there has to be real fear in order to display real courage. As Dr. Perkins often says, courage is not the absence of fear, but moving forward despite your fears.

Jesus waited until it was late at night, until the boat had drifted far out to sea, until the winds had picked up and the waters were choppy. He waited until the environment was optimal for fear.

And then, in order to take fear to its furthest potential, he walked to them on the water. By defying the natural order, he left the disciples no choice but to guess how it was that the natural was ceding to the supernatural. It's no wonder that their best theory was that they were seeing a ghost.

Once Jesus came close enough to be identified, he simply said, "Take courage! It is I" (Matt. 14:27).

Courage. That is what Jesus was trying to build into the inner hearts of his disciples. That was why he brought them to the intersection of faith and fear.

Gary Haugen, in his book aptly titled *Just Courage*, notes that the choice faced by the disciples in this moment is the same choice that we as Christ followers are faced with as well:

> Here is one choice that our Father wants us to understand as Christians—and I believe this is the choice of our age: Do we want to be brave or safe? Gently, lovingly, our heavenly Father wants us to know that we simply can't be both.[1]

Do we want to be brave or safe? In Matthew 14 the choice between safe and brave is represented by a pair of images.

The image for "safe" is the boat. There was nothing fundamentally wrong with the boat. Jesus himself had sent them off on that boat the night before. The boat was a means of transport, and it provided a sense of comfort, stability, and control.

The image for "brave" is the water. Normally it would be a foolish idea to step out into the water, especially in the middle of the night as waves are crashing against the boat. But in this moment, the water represented "brave." Though the water was unknown and unpredictable, it was where Jesus was standing. His presence changed the equation and created a clear-cut choice. Did they want to be safe, or did they want to be brave? Would they cling to the static safety of the boat, or would they move bravely toward Jesus?

Peter is the one who correctly interprets what Jesus is asking for in this moment, and his decision sheds light on the true nature of courage. "'Lord, if it's you,' Peter replied, 'tell me to come to you on the water'" (v. 28).

Jesus's reply is all of one word: "Come" (v. 29). Apparently Jesus believed that Peter had been given enough information to take the necessary step of faith. Now it was up to him to decide whether he wanted to be safe or to be brave.

Peter chose brave and moved toward Jesus with courageous faith. Fear and anxiety were certainly present, yet Peter trusted that somehow Jesus would provide a means for him to walk, even if it wasn't obvious to the naked eye.

Peter stepped out of the boat, placed his feet on the water, and didn't sink! By choosing faith in Jesus over fear of the unknown, Peter experienced the supernatural. Like Jesus, he walked on water.

His flirtation with the supernatural was brief, though. When Peter's gaze shifted from Jesus back to the choppy waters, he started to sink and in desperation shouted, "Lord, save me!" (v. 30).

Jesus was at his side within seconds and lifted him back out of the water. As he pulled Peter out, he asked an intriguing question: "You of little faith . . . why did you doubt?" (v. 31).

Wait a minute—"You of little faith"? Doesn't that seem a bit over the top? Peter was the only one who actually had enough courage to step out of the boat in the first place. It seems that his faith should be commended, not questioned. What about the eleven who stayed back? Why not ask them why they had such little faith?

Clearly Jesus was not making a universal statement about Peter's faith. Peter had proven his love and devotion to Jesus repeatedly. Whatever was happening here was an object lesson on the nature of courage, and that is the lens by which to interpret Jesus's question.

Courage is not something you either permanently have or permanently lack. Courage is a virtue that is developed into the depth of our character by Jesus himself, and it is a direct by-product of our relationship with fear and faith.

Peter was courageous one moment but then lost his courage the next. And while the others lacked courage in that moment, their ultimate legacy would be far different.

It is sobering to reflect on the specifics of how each of them died, but the fact that almost all of them died as martyrs shows just how deep their eventual courage went (Judas was the obvious exception; he took his own life after betraying Jesus). James was killed by sword, while Andrew, Philip, and Simon the Zealot were crucified. Thaddeus (or Jude) was beaten to death with sticks, and Matthias was stoned while hanging upon a cross. Matthew the tax collector was beheaded, and Thomas—the same one who was given the nickname "doubting" Thomas—was stabbed with pine spears, tormented with red-hot plates, and then burned alive for refusing to disavow his commitment to Jesus. James, the brother of Jesus, was thrown off the pinnacle of the same temple where Satan tempted Jesus. And Peter thought himself unworthy to be crucified as his Master was and asked to be crucified upside down.

John was the only one in this group who escaped a martyr's death, but he didn't exactly get to take the easy path either. After somehow surviving being thrown into boiling water, he was exiled to the island of Patmos under the directive of Emperor Domitian for his proclamation of the risen Christ.

The eventual courage they displayed was not something that was formed overnight. Instead, that courage reflects an accumulation of a thousand moments where they met Jesus at the intersection of faith and fear. Moments where they came face-to-face with the choice: Would they be safe, or would they be brave?

Jesus loves you and me the same way Jesus loved those disciples and the same way he loved the rich young ruler. Jesus wants to develop a spirit of courage in us so that we can become men and women who can face our fear and follow Jesus through our fear.

Everything hinges on courage.

When Jesus brings us to the intersection of faith and fear, he does it so that we can take another step toward the courageous life. Sometimes the intersection feels like something small, like being honest at work or saying a kind word to someone who is struggling. Sometimes the intersection feels big, like confronting a broken relationship or giving away an exorbitant amount of money to a cause that God has stirred your heart for.

It's never too late to become a man or woman of courage. In Matthew 14, only one of the twelve disciples took the courageous road, but that didn't mean that it was too late for the other eleven. They would eventually get there. Perhaps the same thing happened to the rich young ruler. Who is to say that he didn't follow in the footsteps of Nicodemus? Nicodemus initially lacked the courage to follow Jesus, yet by the time of Jesus's death, Nicodemus had become bold enough to publicly reveal what he now believed (see John 19:39).

The great longing of my heart is to be known as a man of courage. And courage is the primary virtue that I want to instill into my children. As we develop a deeper sense of courage, we increase our capacity to boldly respond to the movement of God in our lives.

And when we do that, we are finally ready to respond to Jesus as he whispers, "Come, follow me."

Matthew 14 has been the single most important text in my life for understanding the anatomy of courage and for learning how to respond to Jesus when he brings me to the intersection of faith and fear. Here are three important takeaways to consider regarding courage from this text.

Courage Punctures the Illusion of Our Control

The reason fear is so powerful is because it cries out for safety, for comfort, and for security. Fear convinces us that if we will just retreat to the boat, we can retain some level of control over our lives.

But to think like that is not just limiting; it's to buy into a lie. We intuitively sense this, but we need to remind ourselves out loud that pursuing control in our lives is nothing but an illusion. So little in life is actually under our control.

We have no control over the conflicts happening between major countries. We have no control over whether a natural disaster will strike. We have no control over whether a major illness will suddenly seize our body. We have no control over how much alcohol other people consume or how safely they are going to drive.

Even the things we think we have control over eventually give way to reality. We think we are a good employee but unexpectedly lose our job. We think we are a good girlfriend or boyfriend but discover our partner has been unfaithful. We think we are a good parent but watch our child make harmful choices. We think we are on a promising path but see our dreams suddenly shattered.

When Jesus reveals himself to us in unexpected places and in unexpected ways, we do have control over whether or not we respond to him in faith. When Jesus brings us to the intersection of fear and faith, we do have control over whether we choose in that particular moment to be safe or to be brave.

When we choose safety, we miss an opportunity to grow in courage. But when we choose bravery, our character becomes more deeply rooted in courage.

Courage Helps Us Enter into a Fuller Life

While fear sets limits on our ability to experience fullness of life, faith expands the boundaries. That's one of the clearest takeaways from the encounter in Matthew 14. In the middle of all the commotion, Peter had the experience of a lifetime. When he stepped onto the water with Jesus, he experienced the supernatural.

When the disciples got home that night and reflected on the event, what do you think Peter thought about his decision? Do you suppose that he regretted getting out of the boat? Of course not! The fact that he temporarily faltered at the end didn't overshadow that he still had an unforgettable moment with Jesus. If he had chosen safety over bravery, he would have missed that moment. By choosing to courageously move toward Jesus, he was able to get a glimpse of the abundance of God that he otherwise would not have had the opportunity to see.

We recently experienced this principle firsthand in our own community. The "ministry of reconciliation," as the apostle Paul calls it in 2 Corinthians 5:18, is at the center of our vision at River City. This kind of work brings lots of fear and faith moments, as so much painful history must be addressed when moving into a new future together in Christ.

About two months ago, one of the members of our River City leadership team suggested something unique. She said something like this:

> We have come so far in our ability as a leadership team to have hard, honest, and provocative discussions about the ways that race, culture, and economics shape the way we understand the Bible, prayer, community, worship styles, etc. These conversations are so enriching, and we all agree that ultimately they allow us to walk away with a bigger vision of God, church, and faith. So I think God has sparked an idea in me, and I want to throw it out to the group. Why don't we consider having that conversation out loud, in front of the whole community? We could do a one-week experiment—replace the traditional sermon and instead have a group discussion about the way we are working out reconciliation as a leadership team. Then we could see how God uses that to ignite conversations within the body.

This sounded great in theory but was terrifying in practice. Building a multiethnic leadership team has been by far one of the most challenging endeavors within River City. It's one of the facets that I am most proud of, but it's also been the most costly learning curve. The journey toward following Jesus into reconciliation is the epitome of choosing between faith and fear, safe and brave.

Our current team is made up of four whites, four African Americans, one African, two Latino Americans, and two Asian Americans, and even within the different cultural subgroups, there is a tremendous diversity of life experience and perspective. This brings so much joy but also so much complexity. There is no such thing as a simple agenda item when you have that many different perspectives in the circle.

We've spent enough years together that we have finally developed an atmosphere of trust and safety, which is a necessary precondition for having authentic conversations about power, privilege, and the other tense but important topics we need to address in this type of community. We often dive into reconciliation conversations together, and when we do, they are spirited and intense. We've all come to appreciate that intensity, though, as it has been the catalyst for significant growth.

But now one of our leaders was suggesting something that frightened all of us. She was suggesting that we take that conversation out of the safety and comfort of our group and open it up to the entire church community. The fear this suggestion brought was different for each person in the group. Some feared that they would say something culturally ignorant or offensive in front of the whole church. Others feared that being too vulnerable would create feelings of unease from racial groups outside of their own. Still others feared that even if everything was said just right, it would still leave too much possibility of misinterpretation.

We talked through both the potential gains and costs of doing this, as well as the fears it was evoking. We wrestled for months with the idea of doing it and felt stuck. What finally broke the stalemate was the simplest of questions. One of our elders asked, "Do we sense that Jesus is leading us to do this?" We all paused, reflected, and then answered unanimously, "Yes, we believe that Jesus is leading us to do this."

And with that it was solved.

We prayed and planned the best we could, but at the end of the day we all had to acknowledge that we had no idea how this was actually going to go. We had never heard of another church trying something like this, so there was no clear-cut path for what we were trying to do.

All we knew was that it seemed that Jesus was leading us by faith into a new reality as a community, and we wanted to courageously follow. It was time for our leadership team to choose between being safe and being brave, and we decided to be brave.

On that Sunday we sang just one song, and then all thirteen members of our leadership team sat in a semicircle in front of the church. We dove into a deep exploration of how we sensed God was moving in our community, where we believed Jesus was leading us, and some of the risks of following that. We talked honestly about how the ministry of reconciliation had personally affected us in both good and hard ways. We talked about the struggles of reconciliation but also the hope that we saw within it.

The response was fantastic. Our transparency sparked a new level of authenticity within our congregation, and dozens of side conversations are still continuing. People are excited to listen to God together and to celebrate the fact that each one of us has something unique to contribute to what God is doing.

It would have been easy to choose safety when this opportunity came up, and it would have been easy to justify it. But if we had chosen safe, we would have placed restrictions on the fullness of life that Jesus was trying to lead our community into. By courageously following Jesus, even when we didn't know exactly where we'd end up, we have had the boundaries of our experience expanded and enriched.

I can't remember a single time when I courageously responded to Jesus and then found myself regretting it on the other end. That is what I hope will be true for you too. Courage is like a muscle—the more you exercise it, the stronger it becomes. In the early stages of courageously following Jesus, the choice between safe and brave often feels overwhelming. The more of life we have tried to control, the harder it is to choose brave.

But courage has a muscle memory. When it begins to be stretched out, it responds better with each new opportunity to grow. And that is what ultimately turns a person into someone who is genuinely courageous.

Courage Allows Us to Experience Holistic, Multidimensional Faith

We must always keep the big picture in view as we pursue the fullness of life that comes through faith in Christ. It's easy to get so focused on one particular dimension that we forget the importance of the others.

We need to become courageous people in order to follow Jesus through the intersection of faith and fear, but that is not the end of the journey. When Jesus created this moment on the lake as an opportunity for the disciples to learn deeper forms of courage, it was ultimately intended to create a deeper sense of worship. This is how Matthew finished the account:

> Then those who were in the boat worshiped him, saying, "Truly you are the Son of God." (Matt. 14:33)

Courage is never an end in and of itself. Courage is a virtue, nurtured into our character by the author and pioneer of our faith. It is courage that we need if we are to boldly follow Jesus into an ongoing, worshipful experience with the almighty God.

9

///////////////

Pay Attention

Our problem is not to be rid of fear but rather to harness and master it.

Dr. Martin Luther King Jr.

One of the most significant gifts I was given as a young leader was the opportunity to work for a wise and godly woman named Nancy Ortberg. When I left corporate America to work at Willow Creek, she was my first boss.

Nancy played a tremendous role in the shaping of my development as a leader. She helped me to spot and develop many of the latent skills and abilities I had and helped me to put them into practice. But more importantly than that, she relentlessly challenged the development of my character. She had an unwavering belief that emotional health was the most important X factor in having an impact over the long term and in becoming the kind of person who could courageously step into the faith moments that God puts before us.

One of the first character deficiencies that Nancy sensed in me was my inability to identify, harness, and master fear. That fear had such an impact on me was not the big issue—she knew that was part of the human condition. What worried her was my blindness to it. Instead of acknowledging the power of fear, I consistently denied and dismissed it. She worried this would become a significant threat to the spiritual formation that Jesus desired for me, and therefore she looked for ways to drive home this point in my life.

At first she used the soft and gentle approach. She would drop hints and mention the importance of self-awareness in subtle (and not so subtle) ways. Eventually she realized this was going nowhere and decided to upgrade to a more strong-armed approach.

At Willow Creek we would receive an annual performance review, and the process was designed to both affirm areas of strength and map out a strategy for how the employee could improve their areas of weakness. My first performance review with Nancy went great. The review spent much more time cataloging strengths than weaknesses, and I felt very affirmed in the contribution I was making.

But my second performance review was an altogether different story. Nancy started with the strengths and went over a list of ministry successes that seemed impressive on paper. But they were discussed in a sober tone that didn't match the contribution level I thought I had made.

When it came time to address weaknesses, she zeroed in on my lack of emotional awareness and health. Her summary statement said something like this: "Daniel is one of the most talented young adults I've worked with, and he has tremendous potential. Unfortunately, he is also one of the least emotionally aware adults I've worked with, and this will become his ultimate undoing if it is not dealt with."

I was completely caught off guard and immediately became defensive. I admittedly didn't think much about emotional awareness, but I also thought its importance was being overblown. I had come from the corporate world, and emotion had never been given even a passing mention in my evaluations. The bottom line was always whether or not you got the job done. Why then the big deal about emotional awareness in the church workplace?

After my defensiveness began to die down, I started moving toward being dismissive instead. I am kind of embarrassed to admit it, but my thinking was something like this: "It figures it's a woman saying this to me. A guy would never mention emotional awareness/health as part of an employee evaluation. And he certainly wouldn't point to that as the primary criteria that would determine my future success."

This little exercise made me feel better, but I could see that this had become a big deal for her, so I needed to at least try to appease her. The evaluation process had an action plan associated with it, so I asked Nancy what she wanted me to do as a next step. She proposed three sessions with a Christian counselor to explore my emotional world. *Of course that's what she wants me to do*, I thought skeptically.

I gave my best courtesy smile and agreed to go.

Since I had no idea how to find a Christian counselor, she set up an appointment with hers. I will never forget the awkwardness I felt as I arrived for my first session. I nervously entered his office, sat on the couch, and began to clumsily shift back and forth. You would've thought Jack Bauer was interrogating me by how nervous I was. Sensing my unease, he asked me to share why it was that I had set up the session in the first place. I figured since he knew Nancy, I should just be honest. I said, "I am here for one reason. Nancy is my boss, and she made me come. She says I am not emotionally aware or healthy."

He smiled, and after a moment's pause, he followed up with another question. "Okay, thanks for being honest. Do you think you are emotionally aware and healthy?"

"*Yes*," I said, lying through my teeth.

"Great, let's start there. You have two more sessions, so if you're comfortable, maybe you can share some of what you've learned about your emotional world with me. Since fear is probably the number one emotion that affects our faith, why don't we spend the next session talking about that?"

I agreed. And since I was paying for these sessions, I figured I should at least make it worth the while. When I arrived at his office for my second appointment, he asked me how the process had gone.

I triumphantly pronounced the good news I had discovered after a week's worth of reflections: "I thought about fear all week, and I believe I can honestly say that I am not afraid of anything."

My counselor laughed out loud, something I was pretty sure he wasn't supposed to do. After getting his game face back on, he then rebutted my audacious claim. "That is quite a feat if you have gotten to the place where there is nothing that you fear. I don't want to disagree with your assessment—perhaps you are correct. But could I suggest that it is likely you have at least one fear?"

I thought, *Wow, he doesn't even know me, but now he's going to start telling me what I am afraid of? This should be good.*

He continued. "Do you think it's safe to say that you might be afraid of . . . being afraid?"

Thus began my journey of self-awareness.

It took only minimal self-awareness to open the floodgates of fear. The list that I thought was nonexistent now seemed endless.

I was afraid of not getting people's approval.

I was afraid of not being successful.

I was afraid of not having any meaning in my life.

I was afraid that my faith wasn't real.

I was afraid that if I pursued God with reckless abandon, there would be nothing there.

I was afraid that I would be single all my life.

I was afraid that if I did get married, it would end up being to the wrong person.

I was afraid that my favorite TV show would get canceled.

I was afraid of so many things!

It was initially overwhelming to uncover so many sources of anxiety, so much uncertainty, and so many threats to my sense of control. But it also began to usher my life into a new era of freedom. God was urging me to shed the false and put on the real, to stop pretending with him (and myself), and to lay myself bare before him.

I thought this level of transparency would leave me feeling frightfully vulnerable. Instead, it left me feeling known, seen, and loved. God wasn't saying, "Daniel, you're a dreadful coward; please turn away from me." He was saying, "Daniel, you have many fears, but if you have the courage to reveal them to me, I will take you on a journey toward the heart of God that gives you the strength to face any fear." I knew then that the goal of trying to *appear* fearless had to be replaced by a call to *be* courageous.

I was finally beginning to understand just how interconnected fear, faith, and fullness of life are. Though parts of my life felt exciting, I still felt dependent on external success and validation. When I didn't have that, life felt hollow and stagnant.

The Spirit of God was bringing new levels of awareness to the role that fear was playing in that. I was authentically following Jesus, but

I would do so only up to the point where I felt I was losing control. Though many of the things I was doing might appear as risky to outsiders, I knew that they were still within the realm of what was safe for me.

But now that the fears inside of me had found a voice, the ribboned-off areas of my inner life were open to the leadership and love of Jesus. I was finding the courage to acknowledge that much of my false bravado was nothing more than a front for all kinds of hidden fears. By giving those over to Jesus, I was freed to come out of the small world that my soul too often inhabited.

I've become ruthless about identifying fear in my life since then. I want to be a person who is free from fear's power and spiritually agile enough to follow Jesus wherever he wants to lead me. I also want this to be true for others, and therefore the battle between faith and fear has become part of every discipleship conversation I have with people who are aiming to grow spiritually.

When I meet with someone who genuinely wants to grow as a disciple of Jesus and wants to grapple with faith and fear in particular, I start by sharing my favorite quote on the topic, which comes from Dr. Martin Luther King Jr. His writings are filled with wisdom on all three dimensions of faith, but his stuff on fear has particularly impacted me. He said, "Our problem is not to be rid of fear but rather to harness and master it."[1]

This is a helpful framework for addressing the different facets of fear that we have explored in this section. It represents a progression, with each phrase pointing to another important reality about fear:

We need to *honor* the reality of fear.
We need to *harness* the power of fear.
We need to *master* fear.

Honoring the Reality of Fear

The first part of King's quote is the most important, yet the most often ignored: "Our problem is not to be *rid* of fear."[2]

This brings needed correction to one of the most persistent Christian myths about fear. Many of us fall into the same trap that I did for many years. We figure that the best way to try to obey the repeated command to "fear not" is to either suppress whatever feels threatening or unsettling to us, or to pretend like we don't actually have any fear at all.

If we pretend that fear is not there, how will we ever be able to adequately address and master it? Fear has free reign when it is allowed to hide, but it loses its power when it is named and brought into the open.

We also have clearly seen that Jesus intentionally brings us to the intersection of faith and fear on a regular basis. Jesus wants to grow us into men and women who are defined by courage, and that can happen only by taking us up to the boundary of our fears.

We need to remember this, because it goes completely against some of the well-meaning but ultimately unhelpful advice that is regularly passed along within Christian circles: "There is no safer place than the center of God's will."

Have you ever heard this? Part of it is right on. There certainly is no better place to be than God's will. And I think a certain kind of safety comes from following the Good Shepherd that cannot be matched by walking this life on our own.

But this idea gets all mixed in with our desire for security and comfort when it adds the incorrect detail that there is no *safer* place than the center of God's will. That myth is attractive to our base instinct that would prefer to choose safe over brave, but our deepest selves long for something more. What we really long for is adventure, intrigue, and meaning, and that comes only as we choose brave over safe.

Learning to choose brave over safe has become an important value in my community, and we realize that the pull of human nature is always tempting us to reverse that choice. As a way to counteract the powerful current of fear, we have come up with a mantra that we repeat on a regular basis: *You can't "fear not" until you realize you do*.

We recognize that "fear not" is not only one of the most repeated commands—it is also core to the experience of fullness of life. But you can't solve a problem that you don't know you have, and underestimating the powerful presence of fear is a greater threat to our quality of lives than leaning into it and choosing to engage it.

So let's honor the reality of fear in our life and remember that we can't "fear not" until we realize that we already do!

Harnessing the Power of Fear

The second part of Dr. King's quote is also compelling. He doesn't jump right from self-awareness to self-mastery. In between he says we need to "harness" our fears.

What does it mean to harness something? Dictionary.com defines *harness* as "to bring under conditions for effective use; gain control over for a particular end."[3]

I really like that imagery, because you don't need to harness something unless it is powerful. But it also recognizes that because it is powerful, it needs to be controlled. The control is for a purpose—it is controlled for a particular end or for an effective use. It's kind of a good news/bad news type of situation. The bad news is (bad news always goes first, right?), fear is powerful. The good news is, it can be controlled for the greater purposes of following Jesus in faith.

Mastering Fear

First Timothy 4 is a passage that has influenced many young pastors, including me. Here the apostle Paul gives a condensed version of some of the most important leadership lessons that he wants to pass on to Timothy, his cherished protégé. Included in the vision talk is encouragement to embrace his youthful vigor, the importance of pursuing faith rooted in love, the integrity that comes from personal purity, the importance of staying true to core giftedness, and finally, the importance of Scripture.

These are all important lessons to learn, but it's how Paul concludes this section that has had quite an impact on me. In verse 16 he summarizes his lesson with this: "Pay close attention to yourself and to your teaching; continue in these things, for in doing this you will save both yourself and your hearers" (NRSV).

"Pay close attention to yourself." That carries weight as a standalone sentence, but what he adds on the end puts it over the top: "for in doing this you will save both yourself and your hearers."

Wow—can you believe how strongly Paul makes this point? Apparently Paul got nervous when young pastors earned high marks in theology class but low marks in emotional awareness. Imagine that.

If we are to "master" our fears, then we must heed Paul's words to Timothy. We need to "pay close attention" to ourselves.

Referring back to Matthew 14: we need to know our boat. That is the dominant image of the text, and it represents that which competes with the courage that Jesus is trying to instill within our character.

Your "boat" is not necessarily something bad. The boat often represents something that is actually good—such as family, career, friendship, romance, or vocation. It's when the boat becomes central to your desire for safety that it becomes problematic. If Jesus is moving toward you, but you are retreating to the boat, then the boat becomes a stifling factor in your faith.

Most of us are a lot like the rich young ruler. He genuinely loved God and sincerely wanted to grow, but he had not taken into consideration the possibility that Jesus would call him to "leave the boat." For him the boat was his financial security. His identity was hopelessly wrapped up in money, and the prospect of releasing his grip on that identity was too overwhelming for him to consider in the moment.

That is the deep self-knowledge that we all really need to acquire. Can you put a name on your deepest, most fundamental fear?

Do you fear you won't be needed?

That no one will think you're special?

That you won't be loved?

Very few people have any sense of what their fundamental fear is, and that's a shame. For as long as fear is allowed to live in the shadows, it remains powerful. But once we can identify fear, we are already halfway home! We will never again find ourselves in the situation of the rich young ruler. Jesus may move in our life, and he may bring us right up to the boundary of our greatest fear, and we may feel really nervous about it, but at least it won't be a surprise any longer!

I had grown up hearing terms like "discipleship," but I had a narrow definition. When Nancy forcefully confronted my lack of emotional awareness—and particularly my lack of awareness of fear—she was leading me down a path of transformational discipleship. She was teaching me to "pay close attention" to myself, and the results were remarkable.

I began a new journey of self-discovery, which in turn resulted in new depths for my faith, which in turn "affected my hearers," or those I have been given the privilege of ministering to. I was now able to acknowledge, name, and begin to harness many of the fears that had been stifling my faith. I was now able to take new steps toward the fullness of life that Jesus was trying to lead me into.

///////////

As I look back upon the many significant moments where Jesus led me to the intersection of faith and fear, I am filled with gratitude at the equipping I received. Without the admonition to "pay close attention to yourself," I would not have recognized fear's power over my life. Every one of these represents an encounter I had with Jesus at the intersection of faith and fear:

- leaving the safety of Willow Creek to start a new church from scratch
- moving from the predictability of the suburbs to the restless nature of the urban environment
- transitioning from a monocultural, white congregation to a multiethnic, culturally diverse congregation
- leaving the comfort of an affluent community to join forces with the many unknown heroes who have given their lives to fighting poverty in the name of Jesus

Every story is unique, as is every call from God. The story of where Jesus has led me by faith will have a different ring to it than your story will. But where I'm certain our stories are the same is this: Jesus is the author and the pioneer of your life, and one of the primary ways that he will stream your story into the story of God is by consistently taking you through the intersection of faith and fear.

I hope that you will take seriously the words of the apostle Paul—that you will "pay close attention to yourself" (1 Tim. 4:16 NRSV). Have the courage to acknowledge your fear. Be brave enough to recognize the boats that seduce you with promises of safety and comfort. And step boldly toward the One who is life itself.

Part 3

FAITH
AND
INTIMACY

10
////////////////

The Center of Faith

Whatever our situation in life—butcher, baker, candlestick maker—
our deepest and most pressing need is to learn to walk with God.
To hear his voice. To follow him intimately. It is the most essential
turn of events that could ever take place in the life of any human
being, for it brings us back to the source of life. Everything else we
long for can then flow forth from this union.

John Eldredge

Joshua is my prototype for seeing faith in 3-D with clarity and precision. Through faith, Joshua was able to identify and ultimately master his fears (dimension 1). Through faith, Joshua was able to step into a history-changing mission set before him by God (dimension 3). What ultimately enabled both of these was learning to walk with God intimately by faith (dimension 2). God invited Joshua into an experience of spiritual intimacy with these words:

> As I was with Moses, so I will be with you; I will never leave you nor forsake you. (Josh. 1:5)

When God revealed himself to Joshua, it was not as an impersonal, removed deity. God did not demand fear-based obedience. God didn't say, "Either you obey the commands I have given you, or you'll pay the penalty of that disobedience!"

Instead, God saturated the encounter with the language of spiritual intimacy. Every phrase was dripping with the language of connection and affinity.

> As I was with Moses,
> so I will be with you.
> I will never leave you.
> I will never forsake you.

The invitation to spiritual intimacy with God is repeated again at the end of the encounter:

> Have I not commanded you? Be strong and courageous. Do not be afraid; do not be discouraged, for the LORD your *God will be with you* wherever you go. (Josh. 1:9, emphasis added)

Spiritual intimacy with God is the center of Christianity. We see it throughout the Old Testament, the New Testament, and the teachings of Jesus. Spiritual intimacy with God is therefore the center of faith. By faith Jesus pulls us through our fears, and by faith Jesus leads us into mission. But the source and fountainhead of faith remains our spiritual intimacy with God. Spiritual intimacy is best characterized throughout the Bible as walking with God.

The image of walking with God is first introduced in the book of Genesis, and the writer of Hebrews therefore launches his expedition into faith from there as well. In fact, Genesis becomes the primary source material for almost *all* of his teaching on faith. Despite having an abundance of biblical stories to pull from, the writer of Hebrews devotes over half of chapter 11 to stories from Genesis.

The word *genesis* has the same etymological roots as our word "genes," and that becomes particularly important when trying to grasp the nature of spiritual intimacy with God. As human beings we share a spiritual DNA in common, and through the deliberate ordering of the stories in the opening narrative of Genesis, God invites us to understand how that affects our journey toward spiritual intimacy. As the stories of Genesis unfold, we discover that the character of God remains consistent and steadfast, even if the behaviors and responses of those he loves do not. God continues to relentlessly pursue his most prized creation with full abandon. It's what Brennan Manning affectionately refers to as the furious longing of God.

The image that captures the desire God has for spiritual intimacy is found in Genesis 3:

> Then the man and his wife heard the sound of the LORD God as he was walking in the garden in the cool of the day. (v. 3:8)

In Genesis 1 and 2 we see that God creates the Garden of Eden and then gives the entire Paradise over to Adam and Eve to enjoy. God wants them to enjoy the entire breadth of creation and to swim in the fullness of life that they were designed for. At the center of that daily experience in Paradise was an intimate encounter with God described in chapter 3: Adam and Eve would walk with God in the Garden in the cool of the day.

This is one of my favorite pictures in the whole Bible, and it has had a transformative effect on my understanding of spiritual intimacy with God. It became particularly precious to me after my honeymoon on the Hawaiian island of Kauai. Liz and I had the privilege of visiting this magnificent place for ten days after we got married, and I have never forgotten its beauty. There are certain environments that seem to be only a degree or two away from the original Garden of Eden, and Kauai is one of them.

There were many things to see and experience in Kauai, but what quickly became my favorite was when the "cool of the day" would roll in.

The sun came out hot first thing in the morning, and the extreme heat was a magnet for those who were ready to get their tan before heading back home. I was not one of those. My Irish skin has a low tolerance for intense sunlight, so Liz and I would head in opposite directions each morning. She would head for her version of paradise, which was a sunny spot on the beach with a good novel. I, on the other hand, would flee the hot sun and take refuge under a shaded tree, tropical drink in hand.

The heat would remain intense until late afternoon, but then around 5:00 something magical would happen. The winds would begin to shift, and a strong and steady ocean breeze would blow in off the water. This would regulate the temperature to a point of near perfection. It would remain sunny, yet it was no longer hot. It became breezy, but it was not cold.

Everything in the environment seemed to align with this daily window of perfect weather. The brisk wind would send the waves majestically cresting toward the shoreline in a rhythmic fashion that can't be reproduced outside of the real thing. The leaves of the trees would begin to dance in the breeze, and even the birds seemed to sing in concert. The ambiance was perfect.

When I read the description of God walking with Adam and Eve in the cool of the day, I can't help but remember those daily walks we took on Kauai. I imagine that this must have been what Adam and Eve were able to experience every day in Paradise. All of creation was theirs to enjoy, and it was capped off by this incredible daily experience of spiritual intimacy with God.

Many aspects of Paradise were lost when Adam and Eve sinned, but "walking with God" was not one of them. In fact, this image only gains traction as the book of Genesis unfolds.

Take Enoch for example. His is the second story in Hebrews 11, and the writer of Hebrews says that Enoch was "commended as one who pleased God" (v. 5). Wow, those are some great words to be remembered by, aren't they? What amazing act of heroism do you suppose Enoch performed to be remembered with such glowing terms?

Well . . . we don't know that he ever performed a single heroic act. The Bible never mentions any daring mission or incredible leap of faith that Enoch took. The only thing that Genesis tells us about his great faith is that there was a straight line between it and spiritual intimacy with God. The same image from the Garden of Eden is now used to describe Enoch: "Enoch *walked faithfully* with God; then he was no more, because God took him away" (Gen. 5:24, emphasis added).

The imagery doesn't stop with Enoch. Noah is the next hero of faith listed in Hebrews 11. Want to take a guess as to how his life of faith was described in Genesis? "Noah was a righteous man, blameless among the people of his time, and he *walked faithfully* with God" (Gen. 6:9, emphasis added). Once again spiritual intimacy with God is the hallmark trait of faith, and it is couched within the image of "walking" with God.

As the writer of Hebrews continues telling stories of faith, the imagery of walking with God grows in intensity with each character. Abraham is next, and he received the double honor of being invited to "walk" with God and to be called a "friend" of God (see Gen. 17:1; James 2:23; Moses is the only other faith hero in the Old Testament to be described this way). God invited Abraham into a relationship defined by spiritual intimacy, just as he did with Adam and Eve, Cain and Abel, Enoch and Noah:

> When Abram was ninety-nine years old, the LORD appeared to him and said, "I am God Almighty; *walk before me faithfully* and be blameless." (Gen. 17:1, emphasis added)

"Walking with God" continues to be one of the primary ways of describing spiritual intimacy with God throughout the rest of the Bible. For instance, the apostle Paul repeatedly uses this imagery to describe faith and intimacy. He famously said that we "walk" by faith, and not by sight (2 Cor. 5:7 NRSV). This allows us to in turn "walk" in Christ Jesus the Lord (Col. 2:6 ESV), and to "walk" by the Spirit (Gal. 5:16). In Romans 6 he also develops an important connection between the ways faith unites us with Jesus, and how that allows us to "walk" into a new way of life in Christ (vv. 3–4 NRSV). And there are dozens more examples.

This is really exciting news. God doesn't just accept you; he loves you. And God doesn't just love you—he even likes you! He wants you to be able to experience spiritual intimacy with him. To put it in the language of faith, he wants to lead you, by faith, into an experience of spiritual intimacy with God.

But as exciting as this is, it is also at times . . . oh, what's the best word? Challenging? Confusing? Frustrating?

This is how one of my friends shared her struggle with the reality of spiritual intimacy. I think she puts words to what many of us feel when it comes to experiencing this with God:

> The possibility that I can experience that level of intimacy with God sounds awesome. But in my daily life I don't think I would often

describe this as the functional reality of my relationship with God. I love God, and I do my best to obey God. I think God knows that, and I feel secure in my relationship with God. But intimate? I have had a moment here and a moment there where that may have been true. But I wouldn't say that describes my overall relationship with God. I'm not sure I have enough faith for that.

Though my friend was describing her own personal struggle, I think she could have been the designated spokesperson for an entire multitude of spiritually hungry men and women. I have heard some version of this from so many people. They find themselves thrilled by the vision of intimacy with God yet also feel discouraged by how rarely that is their actual experience.

Do you feel that frustration at all? Do you ever feel a disconnect between a vision of intimacy with God and the reality of actually experiencing that vibrant, personal relationship? Do you relate to her feeling that the image of walking with God is an alluring one, yet also feel confusion as to what it looks like to actually step into that experience of sharing intimacy together? Even as we wrestle with this, there is good news to keep us pressing on.

First, you are not alone. Many great men and women of faith—both past and present—have struggled with this as well. I have read detailed journal accounts from spiritual activists like Mother Teresa and Martin Luther King Jr. and mystics like Teresa of Avila and St. John of the Cross that share this same struggle. They longed for this reality of intimacy to be true, trusted that it was God's intent, but struggled during certain seasons to actually experience this.

Second, you can be comforted by the fact that not only is this God's design for you, but it is also the exact place that Jesus is trying to take you. The vision we see in John 10 of how Jesus intends to lead us into fullness of life is saturated with the language of spiritual intimacy. The journey begins with an intimate and specific call by name (see v. 3). Jesus teaches us how to discern his voice and how to recognize his movements (see vv. 4–5). These are all significant details when it comes to intimacy, and they underscore how important faith is to this process. Jesus leads and we follow.

The section is then capped off with a beautiful description of the spiritual intimacy that we are designed for and led into by Jesus: "I know my sheep and my sheep know me—just as the Father knows me and I know the Father" (vv. 14–15).

Knowing that Jesus is leading us toward spiritual intimacy with God is exciting and reassuring. But we still wonder, why does it often feel like such a struggle to experience spiritual intimacy with God?

I think there are two answers to that question, and they are both important. If we want to follow Jesus into the fullness of life as expressed through faith and intimacy, then we need to wrestle with the barriers we face along the way.

Barrier #1: Our Fears and Insecurities

One of the activities I spend a lot of my time on as a pastor is marital and premarital counseling. When I conduct these counseling sessions, I try to bring a healthy dose of both idealism and realism. The idealism is rooted in the beautiful pictures of marriage that God gives us in Scripture: two people who become one under God and who then experience a love and unity that has the capacity to represent the divine. The realism is rooted in the honest struggle of being human: marriage is the act of two imperfect people who are about to enter into a lifetime of consistently crashing into each other's broken and jagged edges.

Does that sound too harsh or even cynical? I hope not. I think it's just realistic. I've sat with way too many couples who are fighting for vibrancy in their marriage to subscribe to some simplistic, Hollywood version of love. Real relationships take work, and so does real intimacy.

When I work with a couple either preparing for marriage or trying to strengthen or fix an existing marriage, I first take them to the foundation. I believe that the Bible says the center of marriage is actually the same as the center of Christianity: intimacy. That is how Genesis 2 described the marriage of Adam and Eve: "And the man and his wife were both naked, and were not ashamed" (Gen. 2:25 NRSV).

The phrase "naked and unashamed" is a powerful description of intimacy. When we hear *naked*, we tend to think first of the physical dimension. While that is certainly part of it, the biblical concept of being naked represents so much more. Naked describes the act of becoming vulnerable before another person physically, emotionally, spiritually, relationally, financially, and in every other way. To be naked is to fully disclose yourself to another person—to share your dreams, your hopes, your excitements, your fears, and your hurts. A married couple can never fully experience intimacy with each other without also being fully naked (and that's why being naked with each other without the commitment of marriage can be so hurtful).

When a couple learns how to be naked and unashamed in front of each other, they develop a strong foundation for intimacy. Both people now feel accepted, and their humanity is honored. Safety permeates the atmosphere because secrets are kept confidential, shortcomings are met with grace, and dreams are cherished and supported.

Of course, learning to be fully naked in front of another person is easier said than done. A multitude of factors make this difficult, including:

- *Our relational history*: Many of us were raised in family environments where intimacy was either absent or distorted. Add to that the frequency with which many of us have been hurt through a previous intimate relationship, and it seems like we start with a lot of strikes against us.
- *Our cultural scripts*: Men in particular struggle with the concept of intimacy, and that is largely due to the cultural cues we consistently receive in our growing up years. In ways that are both formal and informal, we are told that intimacy is a feminine quality and should be avoided on the journey to real "manhood." This becomes a tremendous liability once that "man" is ready to step into a relationship that requires a foundation of intimacy.
- *The risk of vulnerability*: Dr. Timothy Keller says you know you have experienced the intimate feeling of being naked and unashamed when you can vulnerably disclose yourself to another person, and they neither laugh nor yawn. I agree with him, and I see that as the same reason we fear nakedness so much. The prospect of having a loved one see you fully but then respond with either ridicule or boredom can be enough to stop you from even trying. It is a tremendous risk.

These are just some of the many factors that fuel our fear and insecurity around intimacy, and I'm sure much could be added to the list. We are deeply affected by our fears and inhibitions, and these become barriers to experiencing genuine intimacy with another person.

If we already struggle to overcome our fears and insecurities with another person, then how much more of a gap do we have when it comes to intimacy with the divine? At least when I am pursuing intimacy with another person, I can see and hear and touch them. But when developing intimacy with God, we have the additional burden of developing a relationship with a God who is invisible and at times seemingly inaccessible. This only further heightens our fears and insecurities.

This is what we see in the Garden of Eden when God pursues intimacy with Adam and Eve. God is earnestly searching for them, even after they have rebelled, and calls, "Where are you?" (Gen. 3:9).

Adam and Eve don't initially respond to the overture of God. They feel shame from their sin, and all of their fears and insecurities now come rushing to the surface. Adam finally confesses that he is intentionally avoiding God: "I heard you in the garden, and I was *afraid* because I was *naked*; so I hid" (Gen. 3:10, emphasis added).

I'm grateful that this is so clearly spelled out as part of the introduction to our spiritual DNA. I'm not sure we realize the degree to which fear and insecurity affect our ability to respond to the overtures of God. When I am honest with myself, I realize that I am quite similar to Adam when it comes to my fearful disposition. Sometimes my story is similar to his, and my sin and shame cause me to hide from God. Other times my insecurity shows up in a completely different way, and I fear that if I move toward God, he won't actually be there. All of this fear and insecurity is quite problematic when the goal is to experience the joy of walking with God.

When we stay stuck in our fears, we lose the ability to experience the fullness of life that God intends for us. Fortunately, the reverse is true too. When we grow in our capacity to recognize the movement of Jesus in our life, we see that he is already busy at work, challenging those fears in our life. Faith in Jesus doesn't permanently eliminate our fears and insecurities. But when we are cemented to Jesus through faith, we can be pulled through them.

And this is what we really need. We need Jesus to draw us out of our fear and to lead us to the heart of the Father. That is the only place where we are truly and fully known. That is the intimacy that our heart most longs for and that our soul most needs.

This is both the reality and the hope of faith. Our fears and inhibitions will remain viable competitors to the fullness of life that Jesus is trying to lead us into. But when we allow ourselves to be cemented to Jesus by faith, he will pull us through our fears and into new levels of spiritual intimacy with God.

Barrier #2: The Evil One

The Bible is almost uncomfortably clear that there is another reason why we often struggle to see God's pursuit of us and to respond to his overtures for spiritual intimacy with God: *the presence of the evil one.*

Whenever we see the vision of "walking with God" in Scripture, almost always a warning is attached to it. It is a plea to take seriously the presence of the evil one and the fact that the evil one wants to frustrate, attack, and destroy the vision of spiritual intimacy with God.

This was true in the Garden (as we will see in the next chapter), and it was true in John chapter 10. We have referenced the John 10:10 vision for fullness of life throughout this book, but what is the warning that Jesus gives immediately preceding that vision?

> The thief comes only to steal and kill and destroy; I have come that they may have life, and have it to the full. (John 10:10)

The evil one goes by many names in the Bible, depending on the situation. Some of the names given to him are accuser, deceiver, adversary, tempter, and father of lies.

But in John 10, the name Jesus gives to the evil one is simply *thief.* It creates a clear contrast of agendas. Jesus's vision is to lead us by faith into spiritual intimacy with God, and from there into the fullness of life that we have been designed for. The agenda of the evil one is the opposite—he simply wants to frustrate God's agenda. Prowling around like a thief, he looks for ways to steal, kill, and destroy our emerging spiritual intimacy with God.

I am convinced that these are the two barriers we must overcome if we are to experience authentic intimacy with God. First, we must trust in Jesus to lead us past our own fears and insecurities around intimacy. Second, we must trust in Jesus to lead us past the deceptive techniques of the thief who prowls around looking to steal, kill, and destroy God's vision for our lives.

God pursued Adam and Eve in the Garden and asked, "Where are you?" (Gen. 3:9). That pursuit continued through the prophets, the kings, and the priests, and it culminates with the Good Shepherd, who says, "I've come to get you. Follow me and you will experience the fullness of life." Central to the life of faith is coming to believe that this is true and learning how to hear and respond.

Let's learn to trust the One who has called us out of the darkness and into the light. Let's allow him to lead us into that which our hearts most long for: spiritual intimacy with God.

11

////////////////

The Garden

Thrive is a life word; a word full of *shalom*. Thriving is what life was intended to do, like a flower stubbornly pushing through a crack in the sidewalk. It is why we pause in wonder at a human being's first step, or first word; and why we ought to wonder at every step, and every word. Thriving is what God saw when he made life and saw that it was good.

John Ortberg

Have you ever heard of the game "Two Truths and a Lie"? It was originally designed as an icebreaker to help new people introduce themselves to each other, and it continues to remain popular. In the game everyone writes down three statements, and two are supposed to be true and one is supposed to be a lie. The idea is that the process of separating the truth from the lie helps you get to know the person better.

We could play a version of the same game as we get to know God's invitation to an experience of spiritual intimacy. When we enter into the story of our shared genetic code in the book of Genesis, we see that the story revolves around three lies and a truth.

The "truth" remains the same from beginning to end. It's spiritual intimacy, captured in the image of walking with God in the Garden in the cool of the day. It's been really helpful for my spiritual journey to remember that the center of faith never veers away from this truth. This is always what Jesus is trying to lead us toward.

The three "lies" are that which the evil one uses to try to turn our attention away from the truth. Jesus is leading us by faith into spiritual intimacy with God. The evil one spits out lie after lie in hopes of distracting us from or damaging that process.

This is exactly what Jesus builds the vision of fullness of life around in John 10:10. He is the Good Shepherd, leading us to life, which is wonderful. But the thief lurks in the background, hoping to steal, kill, and destroy that life, which is kind of scary.

What are we to make of the consistent biblical warning to beware of the thief? How are we to think of his presence as he attacks the fullness of life that is intended for us? We are going to focus heavily on the influence of the serpent as he tempted Adam and Eve in the Garden, but before we do, perhaps we should talk about the nature of the evil.

C. S. Lewis wrote a famous book called *The Screwtape Letters* that helped a lot of people develop a balanced and healthy perspective on the enemy's plans. The story follows a senior associate of the devil named Screwtape as he mentors his younger nephew Wormwood. In the thirty-one letters that make up the book, he shares detailed advice on how to leverage various temptations in the hopes of undermining the faith of the Christ follower to whom he has been assigned.

In his preface to *The Screwtape Letters*, C. S. Lewis talks about the balance needed when discussing the biblical reality of the evil one. He cautions against the extreme of having an unhealthy obsession with the devil, and he also cautions against minimizing his presence:

> There are two equal and opposite errors into which our race can fall about the devils. One is to disbelieve in their existence. The other is to believe, and to feel an excessive and unhealthy interest in them. They themselves are equally pleased by both errors.[1]

It does seem that most of us tend to move toward one extreme or the other when the topic arises. Some move toward the first error, and virtually "disbelieve in their existence." For this group, talking about the devil sounds primitive and overspiritualized, and it's hard not to go right to a cartoon version of Satan complete with the pointy horns, red tail, and pitchfork.

Others move toward the opposite error and "feel an excessive and unhealthy interest in them." The extreme members of this group can be tempted to think that the devil is behind everything from curse words to bad traffic.

Perhaps you are able to successfully avoid both extremes, but we can all still use some help finding that healthy middle ground. The Genesis story gives us that needed balance.

The evil one comes personified as a serpent in the opening verse of chapter 3, which is a fascinating way to introduce the presence of evil in Paradise. This is coming directly after we are given a detailed account of the magnificence of the Garden. Everything worked together in symphonic harmony—the environment, the vegetation, the wildlife, and the climate. This is what the Bible describes as *shalom*. Everything was working according to its designed purpose, and because of that everything was also flourishing.

Chapter 2 ends with a description of the relationship of Adam and Eve. We see that shalom extends even to humanity. Adam and Eve were free and they were flourishing, just as everything else in the Garden: "Adam and his wife were both naked, and they felt no shame" (Gen. 2:25).

Now, in the very next verse, we are introduced to the evil one, and things will soon devolve: "Now the serpent was more crafty than any of the wild animals the LORD God had made" (Gen. 3:1).

On one hand, this account helps us avoid the mistake of minimizing or ignoring the role that evil plays in our everyday life. Genesis 3 is describing the fall of humanity, and this becomes the theological foundation for the rest of the Bible. If the only factor involved with the fall of Adam and Eve was their sinful actions, then it would make no sense to include the serpent in the story. Clearly the Garden account is showing that we don't live in a vacuum. The evil one knows how easily we are tempted to wander from God, and he regularly throws lies at those temptations in hopes of frustrating our ability to respond to God's pursuit of us.

On the other hand, it also helps us avoid the mistake of overstating or dramatizing the presence of the evil one. If the main point of Genesis 3 was to show how extremely dangerous and powerful the devil is, then you would have expected him to be depicted as something out of medieval folklore. A monstrous dragon or fierce two-headed beast would have certainly done the trick.

Instead, the devil is introduced as a serpent. He is cunning, crafty, and a little bit dangerous, but still . . . he is just a serpent. I mean really, how scary is a serpent? If you see a snake in the wild you certainly avoid it, but you don't cower in fear. The same is true within the broader animal kingdom. If a large predator emerges into plain sight, all the animals go running for cover. But when a serpent slithers out into the open, which animals go running for cover? Field mice?

That's why the serpent's role in the story of the Garden is important. We need a balanced, calibrated approach to the reality of the evil one. We need to recognize that he exists and influences humanity through lies that play to our inner temptations. But we need not cower in fear of him. Faith in Jesus allows us to see through and ultimately overcome his tricks and lies.

This ultimate victory is foreshadowed within Genesis 3. God re-enters the scene after the fall, and though he has a lot to say to Adam and Eve, he barely acknowledges the serpent. You get a sense of the majestic, pervasive reality of God, and then there's this tiny little serpent cowering in the corner. When God's presence is in the same place as the lying serpent, there is no confusion as to who is in control.

When God does address the serpent, it's only to put him in his place. God tells the serpent that he is cursed and that he will meet his eventual doom at the hands of Jesus. In words that must have struck terror into the devil, God simply says, "he will crush your head" (Gen. 3:15). Wow!

Clearly we see that the serpent is no match for the power of Jesus. The endgame has already been set—the serpent's head will be crushed by the majesty of Jesus. We need not live in fear of the devil.

And yet we are most certainly not to ignore him either. He plays a huge role in the story in the Garden, and that is meant to show that he plays a part in our story too. His lies are convincing enough to cause Adam and Eve to question God's character, and they are convincing enough to do the same for us.

When Jesus describes himself in John 10 as the Good Shepherd, he especially highlights the role that faith plays in being able to clearly recognize and hear his voice. Four different times he references the ability of those who follow him to distinguish between the voice of Jesus and the voices of "thieves and robbers" (v. 8).

This is one of the most empowering realities about faith in Jesus. Jesus recognizes the presence of a thief, but then he immediately reassures us that it will be okay. When we listen to the voice of Jesus and follow him, we will be free from the devious tricks of the evil one.

Faith is what allows us to stay connected to Jesus and to follow him into spiritual intimacy with God. Faith gives us the ability to clearly differentiate between the voice of Jesus and the voice of the thief. Faith gives us the ability to pierce the lies of the evil one and to stand firmly in the truth.

When teaching on the Mount of Olives, Jesus said of the devil, "He is a liar and the father of lies" (John 8:44). I have been transformed by discovering that the only influence that the devil really has over me is to lie. He is not all-powerful or all-knowing. He doesn't have anything special to offer to me. He can't provide me a better life.

At the end of the day, there is really nothing at all the evil one can offer you either. All he can do is lie, lie, and lie some more. All he can do is twist and distort and question, and then hope that he can make the straight line to the truth appear crooked.

The evil one loses all power once we are able to accurately identify his lies. When we understand the ways of the "father of lies," we can then learn to clearly differentiate between his deceitful voice and the life-giving voice of the Good Shepherd.

The one "truth" remains the same from beginning to end: it's spiritual intimacy, seen in the captivating image of walking with God. The three "lies" are that which the evil one uses to try to turn our attention away from the life-transforming truth of spiritual intimacy with God. Here is the first:

Lie #1: God is not good.

The father of lies begins his deceitful work by attacking the character of God. He plants a seed in Eve's mind that God is holding out on them, then sits back and watches as it fully blooms.

Now the serpent was more crafty than any of the wild animals the LORD God had made. He said to the woman, "Did God really say, 'You must not eat from any tree in the garden'?"

The woman said to the serpent, "We may eat fruit from the trees in the garden, but God did say, 'You must not eat fruit from the tree that is in the middle of the garden, and you must not touch it, or you will die.'"

"You will not certainly die," the serpent said to the woman. "For God knows that when you eat from it your eyes will be opened, and you will be like God, knowing good and evil."

When the woman saw that the fruit of the tree was good for food and pleasing to the eye, and also desirable for gaining wisdom, she took some and ate it. She also gave some to her husband, who was with her, and he ate it. (Gen. 3:1–6)

Is it surprising to you that Adam and Eve gave in so quickly to Lie #1? How could they so easily question the goodness of God? They had an uninterrupted connection to God, and they had been given an all-access pass to Paradise. They were able to enjoy the world in all of its perfection, and they were able to look directly into the magnificence of God.

How were they so easily deceived into questioning God's goodness? There was only one rule, only one thing they couldn't do. A single tree in the middle of the Garden had a "No Trespassing" sign on it. Why were they so easily deceived into interpreting that prohibition as God holding out on them?

It seems incredible that they could be so easily deceived—until we turn our gaze back to our own walk with God. Don't we fall for that lie just as easily? I can go from "God is incredible" to questioning the goodness of God in an embarrassingly short amount of time.

Have there been times in your life when something happened and suddenly you were getting pulled into a deep, internal struggle about the goodness of God?

Sometimes the catalyst is the magnitude of the suffering in the world. We look at the gap between those who have abundance and those who are in destitute conditions, and we wonder how a good God can let this happen. Or we hear of another case of abuse, of another rape, or of another teenager shot and killed in one of our cities.

Sometimes the catalyst is a tremendous personal disappointment. The death of a loved one, a relational breakup, dashed hopes and dreams—these can all become catalysts for Lie #1 to grab hold of us.

Sometimes the catalyst is something as primal as desire. I often find myself buying into the same temptation as the younger brother in the parable of the prodigal son in Luke 15. Do you remember the story? The younger of two brothers buys into the lie that his father is holding out on him, and he cashes in his share of the inheritance early. He immediately heads out to a "distant country" and spends all his money on "wild living" (v. 13).

We question the goodness of God and instead buy into the belief that the Father is some combination of repressive, dogmatic, boring, and removed. It naturally leads to the assumption that if we are ever going to experience "true" life and freedom, we have to get out of his house.

Not long ago, I was sitting next to a woman on a plane, happily minding my own business. She was intensely reading a book, and every minute or two she would burst out in uncontrollable laughter. I don't usually strike up conversations with complete strangers, but her giddy response to the book was just too interesting for my curiosity to ignore.

I asked her what she was reading, and she was more than happy to not only tell me what it was but also summarize the entire story. She was reading *I Hope They Serve Beer in Hell*, and she claimed it was the best book she had ever read (I had never heard of it, but apparently it was a repeat *New York Times* bestseller and a blockbuster movie).

The book follows the chronicles of Tucker Max, who lives his life with no restraints. He is a man of many carnal desires and believes that no one should have the right to dictate what he is allowed to do or not do. He is the emblem of cultural freedom. If he wants to have sex, he has sex. If he wants to go on an all-night bender, he does it without a second thought. He is unbounded.

The other main character is his best friend, Dan, and Dan is the polar opposite of Tucker. Dan is your run-of-the-mill, everyday kind of person. He works a 9-to-5 job, has a steady life, and lives obediently according to the rules of society. But secretly he wishes he could be more like Tucker, who seems to live life without limits. If Tucker wants something, he takes it, and Dan wishes he were more like him.

Dan gets engaged to a woman named Kristy, and she brings his internal struggle to a head. He values his relationship with her because she fits the vision of a safe, predictable existence that he had always been taught to pursue. She too has been groomed to pursue a controlled, stable life.

But when Dan is around Kristy's mom, he gets a window to what is quickly becoming his greatest fear in life: restriction and joyless existence. The hyper-religious caricature of Kristy's mom could just as easily be Ned Flanders from *The Simpsons*. She is everything you would expect of an ultraconservative fundamentalist. She is plainly dressed, usually annoyed about something, and clearly on the search for anything fun from which she can then immediately extinguish the joy. If Tucker represents freedom, then she represents the extreme opposite: rules, regulations, and joyless duty.

The book essentially asks, Which side will Dan choose? Will he marry Kristy and subscribe to the religious, fundamentalist view of her mom? Or will he break free and live more like Tucker? Will he choose stable, predictable, religious, and boring? Or will he choose freedom, excitement, and an unhindered lifestyle?

As my new friend finished her summary, she was squealing with delight. She said that the book had changed her life and that it had convinced her to break free from the shackles of traditional conservatism. She was now going to live unhindered and free of restraint.

As I sat there listening, I felt like I was being reverse evangelized. The way she told the story was enthusiastic and compelling. Who, after listening to this, would want to live under the constraints of the religious fundamentalism described by the book? They were clearly boring, rigid, joyless, and uninteresting people. And who wouldn't be inspired by the freedom enjoyed by the main character? How fun did it sound to live like Tucker Max, moving from one adventure to the next with no restraints?

As she went back to her reading, I sat there and reflected on the conversation. It didn't take long for me to realize what had just happened and to shake my head at the cunning nature of Lie #1.

The author of this book was simply retelling the oldest lie in the universe. It's the lie that God is not good—that God is more like the joyless, rule-bound, fundamentalist mom in the story. If you want to experience true freedom and true joy, according to the lie, then you have got to do a jailbreak from the confines of this strict and boring God. Whether you are the young prodigal son or Tucker Max or any other archetype of this struggle, there is only one path to true freedom. The enlightened, the bold, the brave—they will be the ones who set out to experience true freedom.

That was the message that this woman was taking away from the book, and she was fully buying into it. She wanted to experience true freedom, and she thought the way to do so was by breaking free from the shackles of religion. I found myself wishing that I could find a way to expose the lie that she was so quickly buying into. I wished I could tell her about my own painful journey and the lies it exposed.

I spent so much of my upbringing being jealous of the Tucker Maxes of the world. When I saw them and their "wild" lifestyles, I was filled with envy. I wished that I could live like them for a while and then get converted right before my life came to an end. It was a distorted way of thinking, but that seemed to be the best of both worlds: sow your oats while you are young, and then come back groveling to God when you've used up the whole bank account of goodwill.

But that is the thing about the lie—it leaves out really important details. Was the younger brother (or Tucker Max, or anyone else living like this) really that free? Was it really the exciting, unhindered, exhilarating, pain-free lifestyle that it gets made out to be?

Of course not. In Luke 15 we see that the younger brother's wild living was short-lived and that he quickly hit rock bottom. He had no friends, no money, and no family. He was competing with pigs for scraps of food. When he finally lost all his strength and returned home, he was completely broken down. Likewise, in Genesis 3 the results of Adam and Eve chasing the mirage of self-independence were extremely painful. They had never been as free as when they were in the presence of God.

I didn't pay attention to this part of the story when I was young, because I figured it was just part of the propaganda. But then something began to happen. I began to see the real-life version of what was consistently described in the Bible. Many of my friends who chose the "wild" path enjoyed it for a while, but many of them ended up crashing and burning at a later point. I have walked with many childhood friends whose lifestyle I initially envied but who now are working their way through the wreckage of divorce, addictions, massive debt, and broken relationships.

It confirmed what I should have already known—Lie #1 is a mirage, and it will take you away from what you most desperately and truly long for. It is only when we are walking with God that we are truly free. It is only when we are walking with God that the true desires of our hearts can be met and the deepest longings that we didn't even know we had can surface.

Not all of you buy into the younger brother version of the lie like I did, but hopefully you have the self-awareness to spot the way it creeps into your life. At the root of Lie #1 is an assault on God's character. It calls into question whether God is really good. It plants the seed of thinking that God is holding out on you and that if you could just get outside of God's grasp, you could find whatever it is he's keeping from you.

The Genesis account shows us how potent the lie is and how quickly we can give into it in both big and small ways. We need the Spirit of God to help us clearly spot the lie in our life and then follow Jesus into the truth.

The most fascinating thing to me about the Genesis account of the first lie is not what God does. It's what God *doesn't* do.

The serpent enters into the Garden and begins to immediately attack God's character. He insinuates that God is intentionally hiding a fountain of wisdom and enlightenment. He questions God's goodness and the motivation behind his commands.

If ever there was a time when God should have intervened, wasn't this it? His reputation was taking a huge hit! And Adam and Eve were clearly faltering. Why not step in and stop the nonsense?

The lack of intervention is made even more pronounced by how present God is immediately before the lie and immediately after. While God's presence is clear and tangible to Adam and Eve on either side of the temptation, they do not hear a single word from God *during* the temptation.

The exact moment when the serpent is calling into question whether God is good and whether Adam and Eve are free is the exact moment when God's goodness and God's commitment to freedom are most clearly seen. If God had intervened during this temptation, even a little bit, then we would have discovered that Adam and Eve were never truly free. Instead, they would have been actors in a controlled environment, manipulated toward desired outcomes and behaviors.

But that is not what we see. God created Adam and Eve to be free. He knew that this was what they were designed for, and he knew that this was the only way they could have true intimacy. Intimacy and freedom are always intertwined. They could not be free to love God without also being free to reject God. They couldn't be free to move toward God without also being free to move away from God.

That is where I can see God's goodness just jumping out of the pages. God was so good, and so committed to freedom, that he chose to sit back and watch as those he most loved chose to reject him.

God demonstrated the goodness of his character before the tempta- tion, and God demonstrated the goodness of his character after the temptation. But in between, God refused to meddle.

The price God paid for us to be free—the price God continues to pay for us to be free—is astonishing.

Some people see the freedom that God has given us as a reason to question the goodness of God. But without freedom there is no love, no intimacy. C. S. Lewis sums this up nicely:

> God created things which had free will. That means creatures which can go either wrong or right. Some people think they can imagine a creature which was free but had no possibility of going wrong; I can- not. If a thing is free to be good it is also free to be bad. And free will is what has made evil possible. Why, then, did God give them free will? Because free will, though it makes evil possible, is also the only thing that makes possible any love or goodness or joy worth having. A world of automata—of creatures that worked like machines—would hardly be worth creating. The happiness which God designs for His higher creatures is the happiness of being freely, voluntarily united to Him and to each other in an ecstasy of love and delight compared with which the most rapturous love between a man and a woman on this earth is mere milk and water. And for that they must be free.[2]

One of the ways that Jesus leads us into life and away from death is by helping us to see this truth through the eyes of God. We are created to be free, and it is that freedom that creates the foundation for genuine intimacy with God. If we are going to learn that we are truly free to walk with God, we must also learn that we are free not to.

12

///////////////

Independence Day

God operates in love by faith. If we do not understand His love we have no foundation for faith. If we do not understand His requirement of faith it will affect our understanding of His love.

Rex Rouis

The second lie in the Garden is the big one, and one could argue that it is at the root of all other sin. It is what one of my favorite Bible teachers calls Adam and Eve's "personal Independence Day."

We have already observed how the serpent spun the first lie. He attacked God's character, and in doing so he caused Adam and Eve to question the goodness of God. Now the serpent is going to take it up a notch as he lays the groundwork for Lie #2. He tells them that if they eat off of the forbidden tree, they will "be like God."

> "You will not certainly die," the serpent said to the woman. "For God knows that when you eat from it your eyes will be opened, and *you will be like God*, knowing good and evil." (Gen. 3:4–5, emphasis added)

The lie is so bald-faced and presumptive that it is hard for me to even repeat out loud. That's what makes this lie both dangerous and difficult to understand. When I first came in contact with Lie #2, that I would be "like God," I struggled to see how it applied. I have never uttered words like that in my whole life. Even when I was far from God, I never walked around saying, "I wish I could be more like God. That would be so awesome."

I wouldn't be surprised if you're having the same reaction to this part of the text. When it comes to spiritual intimacy with God, I am trying to figure out how to be closer to God, not how to *be* God. For some reason it was a temptation for Adam and Eve, but that can't possibly be what's keeping me from the experience of spiritual intimacy I long for, can it?

I just happened to be having lunch with one of my mentors during the time I was thinking about this text for the first time, and I shared with him my struggle to find myself in the story. I told him that I was pretty certain that I was exempt from Lie #2—there didn't seem to be any part of me that was trying to be like God.

I will never forget his response: "I'd be careful not to let yourself off the hook too quickly. Maybe the ways that you 'play God' are not immediately obvious to you. But if this lie was able to derail Adam and Eve, who knew and loved God, then it should be taken seriously. And don't forget—it was also that same lie that ultimately caused Satan to fall from heaven."

It was that second part of his statement that especially grabbed my attention. I had never thought about the fact that Lie #2 was not just the pinnacle of the Garden temptation; it was also the lie that ignited Satan's rebellion against God.

The Bible does not give us extensive details on the backstory of Satan, but what it does tell us is very informative. Before his fall from grace, Satan was a majestic and beautiful angel. Ezekiel 28:12 describes him as "perfection, full of wisdom and perfect in beauty." He was also referred to as a "guardian cherub" (Ezek. 28:16), which indicates that he had an ascendant position within heaven. Cherubim or cherubs are angelic beings, and the Bible typically describes them as the ones most involved in the worship and praise of God. As one of the "guardians" of this group, Satan had the job of not only worshiping but quite possibly leading the charge. The important takeaway is that Satan had a firsthand glimpse into the wonder, majesty, and heart of God.

But instead of that access to God's presence leading to a state of ongoing worship and humility, Satan ran in the opposite direction.

His desire was that majesty and splendor would be his alone, and he led a mutiny against God. The most elaborate description of his insubordination and ultimate secession is found in Isaiah 14:13–14:

> You said in your heart,
>   "I will ascend to the heavens;
> I will raise my throne
>   above the stars of God;
> I will sit enthroned on the mount of assembly,
>   on the utmost heights of Mount Zaphon.
> I will ascend above the tops of the clouds;
>   I will make myself like the Most High."

Satan's final words before his cosmic fall were, "I will make myself like the Most High," and they sound eerily similar to the heart of the second temptation. There is something about this lie—that we can declare our independence and "be like God"—that appeals to a broken part of humanity. We easily confuse the Creator with the created, the Designer with the designed, the Image with the model.

So what does that look like? How is it that the temptation to "be like God" plays out in our lives? And how is it that this lie affects intimacy?

The most obvious and expected way that Adam and Eve played God was by disobeying God's command. Against the backdrop of endless abundance, they were given only one rule: don't eat of the tree in the middle of the garden. When they chose to defy that command, it was a bold power play for independence. Then, to compound things, they found ways to rationalize and justify that disobedience (check out Gen. 3:12–13 to see how easy it was for them to blame everyone but themselves).

While this first one is straightforward, it is still important to acknowledge. We will always feel the temptation to push against the boundaries given to us by God, and when we redraw the lines, it is an act of independence from God. Obedience and intimacy are interlinked throughout the Bible (see Exod. 19:4–5 for a great example of this), so the choices we make really do affect intimacy with God.

There is also a less obvious but potentially more debilitating way that we play God. Here is how the serpent got the second lie past Adam and Eve's defenses and into the heart of their true temptation.

He says, "God knows that when you eat from it your eyes will be opened" (Gen. 3:5).

What does it mean that "your eyes will be opened"? What internal desire was the serpent appealing to when he said that?

When we look ahead to the end result of their eating from the forbidden tree, we get needed insight into that question: "Then the eyes of both of them were opened, and they realized they were naked; so they sewed fig leaves together and made coverings for themselves" (Gen. 3:7).

Their eyes were opened, just as the serpent promised, but what they were searching for was not what they found. The big discovery in their newly enlightened state of being was that without God, they were absolutely naked. They instinctively looked for ways to hide this fact and feverishly began patching together fig leaf outfits to cover themselves up.

And with that we see what the temptation was really about. The only way that the serpent could convince Adam and Eve to take such drastic measures against the God they loved was by convincing them that God was shielding them from some deeper spiritual reality. According to Lie #2, there was something about their desire for significance or meaning or security that was being hidden from them by God. According to Lie #2, there was something about the deepest elements of their identity that could not be expressed as long as they were living surrendered to God.

This was groundbreaking for me in my own spiritual walk with God. When I heard the words "be like God," I had trouble seeing how that could possibly represent a significant temptation for me. But when I looked at the inner craving that pushed them to that point—the hunger for meaning, significance, security, and identity—I finally was able to identify.

God speaks to all of us in different ways. I am somewhat embarrassed to admit where it was that the significance of this lie became a blazing hot reality in my spiritual life. It was when I saw the movie *Titanic*.

Yes, I liked the movie *Titanic*. Yes, I saw it in the theater . . . many times. Yes, I endured endless teasing from my friends. But I've made peace with the fact that one of my greatest spiritual discoveries came from such a cheesy film. My wife says that I have the spiritual gift of finding deep meaning in shallow movies, and I am afraid she may be right. Give me a Nicholas Sparks movie and I am certain I can extract the true meaning of life from it. But hey, if God could use a donkey to speak to Balaam, then he can use *Titanic* to speak to me.

In case you never saw it, here is the quick summary. The movie follows seventeen-year-old first-class passenger Rose as she boards the *Titanic*, the large and luxurious passenger liner that famously sank in 1912. We discover that Rose is distraught by her engagement to Cal, a wealthy aristocrat who is heir to a steel fortune in Pittsburgh. Rose's mother has pushed her into the engagement so that they can maintain a high-class status that is now in jeopardy after her father's death left the family debt-ridden. But Rose, feeling trapped, is bucking against both her mother and Cal. She wanders out to the ship's stern and entertains the thought of jumping overboard.

That is when she meets Jack, a young drifter from Wisconsin who won his third-class ticket in a poker game. Jack is from a completely different social class than Cal or Rose, and his very presence becomes appalling to Rose's mother. Yet Rose is strangely drawn to Jack. He is everything that Cal is not—he is unassuming, adventurous, and overflowing with love for life. These qualities ignite Rose's passions, and she feels like she is coming back to life. This places her squarely between two worlds. Does she stay engaged to Cal and lock herself into the security that comes with his social status? Or does she follow her heart and allow herself to get swept into the exciting but potentially unstable way of life that Jack represents?

I know this sounds crazy, but when I saw the movie for the first time, I felt an overwhelming sense of the presence of God. I had to watch it a few more times to figure out what it was that God was telling me (or so I told myself). What eventually became clear to me was that the two love interests that Rose was torn between represented the two different paths for my life.

The first path was represented by Cal. If he could have a Bible verse that summarized his life, it would be Mark 8:36: "What good is it for someone to gain the whole world, yet forfeit their soul?" That was Cal. He had gained that which the world values—money, prestige, and social standing. And yet he had no soul; he was arrogant, controlling, and detached from anyone or anything that fell under his social class. Though he consistently projects an image of strength and significance, it is clear throughout the movie that he struggles with a deep sense of emptiness and desperation.

This struck a nerve with me. I was at a critical crossroads in life, and I was making decisions about what kind of a person I was going to become. I was twenty-two years old, and for the first time I was beginning to feel like I was gaining that which the world deemed "success." Though I was not wealthy yet, I was on a trajectory toward upward mobility. I had joined an internet start-up that experienced booming growth, and I was prepared to leave and start my own company. The technology field was growing at a rapid rate, and I was poised to follow the current and build a thriving business.

This was pulling me down a path that looked a lot like Cal's. It was becoming clear that my intense desire for "success" was a clumsy attempt at covering the yawning emptiness inside of my soul with piles of fig leaves. I never cared about the money—it was simply a means to an end. What I really cared about was trying to prove to people that I mattered.

My family grew up in a poor, working-class neighborhood, and that played a role in my journey. I'm sure there are many working-class neighborhoods that exude a sense of pride in what their families do, but that wasn't true for the circles I was in. My friends, and the families they came from, often described our hometown in derogatory terms. "Nothing good can come from here," a friend's dad would often mutter. This only played up the deep sense of insecurity that I already felt. Even as a boy I struggled with existential questions: "Do I matter? Is there anything special about me? Is there anything unique about me? Will I ever do anything of significance?"

Usually I felt like the answers to these questions were *no*.

Then, as a nineteen-year old, I stumbled into the opportunity to work at Spiegel, a large design firm in the suburbs of Chicago. I was intimidated working in this fast-paced corporate environment and initially feared that I wouldn't be able to cut it. But over time I found my way, and within a year I had established myself as one of their most valuable employees. Receiving consistent praise in the workplace was like pouring water on a parched soul, and I quickly became addicted. I began to set my sights on acquiring more of what I was already experiencing at Spiegel. I wanted to make money, climb the corporate ladder, and show everyone how I had languished as an undiscovered and undervalued talent.

Then I go and see this stupid movie *Titanic*, and God uses it to shake me from the inside. I'm sure I had seen many movies with a character like Cal before, but they had never seized my imagination like this. Every time I would watch the movie, it was like I could hear God say, "That is the path you are on right now. You think the only way you can find a sense of meaning, significance, and identity is through accruing wealth and leapfrogging into a higher social strata. Is that really the path you want to go down? Is that really who I am calling you to become?"

It was such a bizarre and unsettling experience. All thirteen times that I saw the movie in the theater (yes, thirteen), I had the same experience. I would watch Cal's character on the screen, and I would begin to shift in my seat. In fact, a couple of times I became so uncomfortable that I needed to get up and watch from the back of the theater. Each time I felt like I was caught in a Charles Dickens novel, watching the ghost of my future self on the screen.

Jack Dawson's character, on the other hand, was different in every way from Cal's. Jack had nothing that the world values—he had no money, no social status, no 401(k), and no life plan—yet he was the one who possessed an authentic and strong sense of self.

The contrast between their characters comes to a head when Jack is invited to a dinner with the first-class guests. Cal is supposed to be the one who knows this world, but his superficial and controlling personality make him eminently unlikeable. But it is Jack who charms the table with his witty and wise comments.

Rose's mother can barely hide her contempt for Jack and begins asking a series of pointed questions designed to expose his lack of social status. Once it becomes clear that he has no permanent home, is on the boat only because he won his ticket at a lucky poker hand, and has no plan for future employment, she assumes the point has been made clear for everyone to see. She asks the crowning question—the one that she assumes will cause him to cave into shame: "And you find that sort of rootless existence appealing, do you?"

Instead of getting into a war of words, he simply smiles and responds,

Well, yes, ma'am, I do. . . . I mean, I got everything I need right here with
me. I got air in my lungs, a few blank sheets of paper. I mean, I love wak-
ing up in the morning not knowing what's gonna happen, or who I'm
gonna meet, where I'm gonna wind up. Just the other night I was sleep-
ing under a bridge and now here I am on the grandest ship in the world
having champagne with you fine people. I figure life's a gift and I don't
intend on wasting it. You don't know what hand you're gonna get dealt
next. You learn to take life as it comes at you . . . to make each day count.

With that all the guests hold up their champagne glasses and collectively shout, "To make it count!"

I'm pretty certain that James Cameron did not write *Titanic* with
the hope it would provide a vision for life in Christ, but that is exactly what it did for me. It gave me a direct window into Genesis 3
and helped me to understand the lie and the truth in ways that had
previously eluded me.

Lie #2 is that we could be "like God." If someone would have asked
me during this era if there were any ways that I was trying to play
God, I would have confidently declared, "Absolutely not!"

But now I was starting to realize that I was less immune to Lie #2
than I had first thought. In actuality I was walking down a path that
looked strikingly similar to the one Adam and Eve went down. For
me it wasn't about a garden and forbidden fruit but about a budding
career and a quest for self-actualization. The issue was never whether
it was good or bad to earn lots of money—I know many people who
have been called by God to be creators of wealth, and the kingdom of
God advances mightily through their generosity. The issue was where
I was going to look for meaning and identity. Would I look to God
for my sense of identity, or would I declare independence and set off
on my own self-driven quest to find it?

Are you able to find your story within the story of Adam and Eve?
Are you able to see ways in which your temptations to believe Lie #2
resemble their temptations? Remember, this is not the story of two
spiritual seekers on a quest to find God. This is a story of two people
who loved God with all of their hearts. They were experiencing deep
intimacy with God, and yet they still fell victim to the temptation to
play God. They didn't just break the rules—they went on an intentional search for meaning and identity outside of God.

I think this is a pattern that every Christ follower inadvertently slips into from time to time. When I was processing this with my counselor, he gave me a simple but pointed exercise to hold up to myself as a mirror. He told me to take out a journal and to write down what I felt like was the authentic way I would complete this sentence: *In order to be loved, I need to be _____.*

Honest self-reflection is what helped me discover that my answer to that was "successful." I was just like Cal's character in the movie. I was certain that if I could just gain that which the world valued, I would finally be seen as important and given the love and attention I desired. But now I was realizing that it was nothing but smoke. What Jesus said is absolutely true. "What good is it for someone to gain the whole world, yet forfeit their soul?" (Mark 8:36).

How would you finish that sentence? "In order to be loved, I need to be _____." Pretty? Wealthy? Married? Have kids? Advancing in my career? Artistically renowned? Maintaining a certain lifestyle? Needed? The funny guy? With a hot girlfriend?

There are so many ways that we fall into the trap of Lie #2. And it's not always as clear-cut as breaking the rules and eating off of the tree. Many times it is far more subtle and subversive. We give in to the lie that we can only find meaning and significance when we take things into our own hands.

This is one of the reasons we all so badly need to be cemented to Jesus by faith. The Garden account shows us that we will never be free from the lie that we should go on this search for meaning and significance independent of God. Instead of attaching ourselves to Christ and allowing him to lead us, we grab on to the reins and invite Jesus to join us for the ride. The difference between those two is nearly impossible to quantify.

I think this is what Jesus was getting at when he taught the disciples how it is that they find their true selves: "For whoever wants to save their life will lose it, but whoever loses their life for me and for the gospel will save it" (Mark 8:35).

If we go searching for "life" independent of God, it doesn't really matter if we invite Jesus on the journey or not. It is a dead end. Paradoxically, if our search for the abundant life and our true self is not led by Jesus, we end up losing the very thing we so badly crave.

But if we allow Jesus to be the one who leads this journey, we experience the paradox in reverse. We initially have the sense that we are losing our life, but eventually we come to discover that what we are losing is not anything we actually needed in the first place. What we lose is our self-driven ambitions, our narrowly focused dreams, and our inhibitions and fears. Once we allow Jesus to shake us free from those, he can lead us down a path that results in truly finding that which we most long for.

At the end of the day, this whole thing is all about intimacy. The God we love is a good God. God knows that in order to fully bloom into the amazing men and women we are designed to be, we need an atmosphere of trust, safety, and freedom. We are most happy, most alive, and most free when we come into God's presence "naked and unashamed."

This is the place Jesus is always trying to lead us back to. It is not some mysterious, elusive state that we can only dream of from afar. It is meant to be our default, everyday, foundational reality in God.

There is nothing more wonderful than the knowledge that you don't have to pretend with God. The amazing news is more than the fact that God fully sees you in your current state (and even more accurately than you do). The amazing news is that God not only sees you as you are—he even sees you for what you can *become*. God wants you to know that there is infinitely more to you than you can even see right now.

When you and I go searching for meaning and significance independent of God, we frustrate the very thing we most long for. But when we trustingly follow the Good Shepherd to the heart of God, we find the spiritual intimacy we need. We are reminded that we are created in the image of a perfect God. We are reminded that by faith in Jesus, we are sons and daughters of the almighty God. We are reminded that there is still more to come—more than we can even dare to imagine.

Faith is the means by which Jesus takes us into that intimate, secret place within God. And there is nothing more life-giving in the world than being in that place.

13

The Butterfly Effect

There is no need to mince words. I believe that Christianity happens
when men and women experience the reckless, raging confidence
that comes from knowing the God of Jesus Christ.

Brennan Manning

Have you ever heard of the butterfly effect?

It stems from chaos theory, which studies the relationship and interconnectedness of the different elements of our universe. One common application of chaos theory is in the prediction of weather patterns in meteorological circles.

A scientist named Edward Lorenz is the first one to have used the label "the butterfly effect" to describe this particular phenomenon. In December of 1972 he gave a landmark speech at the American Association for the Advancement of Science in Washington, DC. His entire speech revolved around one question: Does the flap of a butterfly's wings in Brazil set off a tornado in Texas?

Lorenz suggested that the whole universe is so integrated and connected that when a butterfly flaps its wings in Brazil, it can affect the climate not just in Brazil but also in Texas.

You could argue that the butterfly effect is the reason that the writer of Hebrews leans so heavily on the book of Genesis when developing the richest description of faith in the Bible. If the flap of a butterfly's wings in Brazil can have implications for Texas's climate, then to what degree does the fallout from the lies of the Garden affect our ability to walk intimately with God?

The writer of Hebrews wants us to observe the clear relationship between our past spiritual history and our current spiritual reality. We share the same spiritual DNA as Adam and Eve—not to mention Cain and Abel, Enoch and Abraham, and so forth. Their story is our story, and our story is their story. Our genetic code is designed for spiritual intimacy with God, but it is easily derailed by the series of temptations and lies that began in the Garden.

The first two lies, which we've already examined, set the stage. They come directly from the mouth of the serpent and plant the seed that leads to Adam and Eve breaking their covenant with God. From there we see the Genesis version of the butterfly effect. Until then, Adam and Eve had exclusively experienced goodness and grace from God, and they had been given no reason to question God's character. But after they sinned, they gave in to Lie #3. The third lie is wrapped up around rejection—it tells us that if we reject God, then God will in turn reject us back.

This final lie comes not from the words of the serpent but from the fear and anxiety produced by Adam and Eve's failure to keep God's commands. For Adam, Lie #3 is revealed in his response to God: "I heard you in the garden, and I was afraid because I was naked; so I hid" (Gen. 3:10).

Lie #3 is, in my opinion, the most spiritually debilitating of all. Lie #3 speaks to the deep-seated fears that every human being already carries when it comes to intimacy: the fear of rejection and/or the fear of abandonment.

If the heart of intimacy is to be "naked and unashamed," then it makes sense that our fear would be tied to the potential of the reverse happening. The possibility of being "naked and *ashamed*" is a terrifying prospect for anyone seriously considering the possibility of intimacy.

When someone is given the gift of seeing you in a vulnerable, au-thentic place, they immediately inherit a tremendous amount of power.

If what they do with that power is either laugh (meaning they don't take you seriously) or yawn (meaning they are uninterested), you will ultimately feel rejected. That is what leads to the feeling of being naked and ashamed, and it represents one of the scariest propositions for any person who longs for true intimacy.

The fear of human rejection that we already carry is exponentially magnified when it comes to the possibility of spiritual rejection. This is what Adam and Eve were battling against in the Garden. Once they have sinned against God, they feel naked and filled with shame, and they now wonder if God has rejected them. They are afraid, so they hide.

This is what many of us do in human relationships. We sense someone moving close to us but fear the possibility of being truly naked and vulnerable. So instead of reciprocating the intimate gesture, we go the exact opposite direction.

We run.

We hide.

We avoid.

This is the fear that Lie #3 builds upon. Lie #3 comes in the form of a whisper in our ear that because we have rejected God, God has now rejected us. It is the lie that tries to convince us that God is distant or that God does not want to be with us.

That is why the Genesis account is so sacred. The sequence of events is so important, and through it God speaks powerfully to both the lie and the truth. So, let's review.

Scene 1: God creates Paradise and tells Adam and Eve to enjoy it fully. God tells them that there is just one tree they are forbidden to eat from and that if they disobey him, they will die (see Gen. 2:15–25).

Scene 2: The serpent appears and tempts them with a pair of powerful lies (see Gen. 3:1–5). Lie #1 attacks the character of God and plants the seed that God is not good. Lie #2 builds on that assumption and then tempts them to pursue meaning and identity outside of God. He promises that if they eat from the tree their eyes will be opened, and they will be "like God" (Gen. 3:5).

Scene 3: Eve decides that the fruit is good, pleasing to the eye, and can provide her with the wisdom she desires, so she takes some and eats it. She also gives some of the fruit to Adam, and he eats it too (see Gen. 3:6–7).

Let me ask you this: What is your recollection of what happens next? Or maybe the better question is, what do you think *should* have happened next?

My best recollection of the story matched my susceptibility to Lie #3. It is tempting for me to assume that my rejection of God leads to God's rejection of me, and that is what I have often read into the Genesis account. After Adam and Eve defied and disobeyed God, my expectation was that the holiness and wrath of God would be unleashed on them. This is the God I remember being taught about growing up—the God who cannot be in the presence of sin; the God whose holiness and wrath are like a burning fire that must be addressed before we can ever come near.

But is that what happens?

No. Following Adam and Eve's rebellion, God's response is so unexpected. The response of God is saturated with grace and love.

> Then the man and his wife heard the sound of the Lord God as he was walking in the garden in the cool of the day, and they hid from the Lord God among the trees of the garden. But the Lord God called to the man, "Where are you?" (Gen. 3:8–9)

What does God do in response to the rebellion of Adam and Eve? God enters the Garden and shouts, "Adam! Eve! Where are you? It's time for our daily walk" (see Gen. 3:9).

What? How is that even possible? They've just spit in the face of God by doing the one and only thing they were commanded not to do. If ever there was a time for God to break out the stick, this is it, right? But that's not what happens. God lovingly, intimately, warmly moves toward them. They are sinful, broken, confused, and running. They have rejected God, yet God does not reject them. There will be a number of aftereffects from Adam and Eve's disobedience, but God rejecting them is not one of them.

Here we get absolute clarity about the true nature of God. We see the lie, and we see the truth.

The lie is that God has rejected us. The lie is that God is distant from us. The lie is that God is punishing us for our sin.

We have so much trouble believing that this is really not true, and it sparks all kinds of questions: What about the consequences of sin? Is there such a thing as healthy shame? Don't we push God away when we reject him?

These are all important and relevant questions. It is clear in Scripture that God longs for our hearts to be soft in remorse before him, to be receptive to his leadings, and ultimately to be fully his.

But the primary focus of this account is not who we are but who God is! God is there, even when we have gone rogue. God is available, even when we are not. God is waiting in faithfulness, even when we are scurrying away into the dark corners of our souls.

Though our actions may affect how close or how distant we feel, we can be sure of one thing—the response of God is always the same. No matter what depths of darkness we have clung to or what height of personal glory we have tried to attain for ourselves, God is there. God is waiting faithfully for us . . . always. It doesn't matter if we are having a good day or a bad day. Tenderly, relentlessly, God continues to come after us.

That truth is like industrial grade steel. It is so powerful that it can cut through any fear, hurt, or doubt. It can transform the human heart and reorient our very sense of identity.

Which is exactly why the third lie is so dangerous and why it must be ruthlessly extracted. I have watched this lie wreak havoc in so many people's lives.

Take my friend Debbie for instance. I will always remember the first time she came to our church. Her posture had an intensity that suggested her pursuit of God was a life-and-death matter. During the sermon her eyes were locked on to the speaker, taking in every word. During worship she had tears streaming down her face. She was clearly desperate to meet and encounter God, and her determination continued each and every week.

When we finally got an opportunity to meet up for coffee, I remarked how I admired the intensity with which she entered into the corporate worship experience each week. She said, "If you knew my story, you would understand why. My father was a Hell's Angel, and I grew up in a biker gang in California. It was like something right out of *Sons of Anarchy*. It was a godless culture. We made up our own rules and lived by our own code. It was a crazy lifestyle, and I have seen things and done things that you would never believe."

She went on to share some of the more colorful chapters from her life and how it was that she came to Chicago and started to attend our church. She described some of the ways she had been impacted by our community and shared some of the important spiritual truths she was learning.

It was a wonderful conversation, and I thought I was following her story. When she finished sharing I jumped in, wanting to encourage her, and said, "Debbie, I'm so glad that you have found and experienced God's love and that it has had such an impact on you. It makes me so happy to hear stories like that."

Her response surprised me. She started to shake her head as tears formed. "I wish that was true. I wish I could say that I found the love of God. But it's too late for me."

Confused, I asked her what she meant. I said, "Debbie, I see how intensely you worship and listen every Sunday. I just listened to you talk about how much you vibe with our community. I can see how honest and authentic you are with your faith. How is it that you can say that you haven't found the love of God or that it's too late for you? I don't understand."

Her response was heartbreaking. "I told you, I have seen things and done things that can never be taken back. It is uplifting for me to participate in a community like this where people have given their lives over to God. But there is no way that God could ever forgive me for what I've done. Even God's grace isn't big enough for someone like me."

There it was—the lie in full effect. Debbie was convinced that God had looked over her track record and delivered a final verdict: *guilty*. No matter how many Bible verses she heard or how many church services she attended, she was convinced that God had permanently and unequivocally rejected her.

Can you identify with her story at all? I've met with a lot of people who struggle with some version of the lie much like Debbie. A little voice whispers that they've done too much, or not enough. It tells them that they are second-class citizens in the kingdom of God and that they will never deserve the love and grace of God.

It's an absolutely terrible lie. I hate it on a visceral level because of the damage it causes in a human life.

Let me tell you one more story. The station of life, the specific struggle, and the details of this story are all different from Debbie's. And yet it is the exact same lie wreaking havoc in the life of a person who loves God but who is suffering from the curse of its butterfly effect.

I preach often on the importance of faith, and specifically on the ability that faith gives us to experience spiritual intimacy with God. During one of my sermons on this topic, I focused particularly on the famous picture of spiritual intimacy in Revelation 3:20: "Here I am! I stand at the door and knock. If anyone hears my voice and opens the door, I will come in and eat with that person, and they with me."

In ancient culture the lack of electricity meant that once the sun went down there was nothing left to do, so to invite someone over for a meal was to do more than just share food. It was to invite someone into an intimate family space and into the full rhythm of that family's life. Since the meal was the central event in the life of a family, in this verse Jesus is saying that he wants to be invited into the inner depths of our lives. I closed the service by pleading with people to open their eyes to the significance of the invitation.

I had hardly said "amen" before Joe came up to the platform to grab me. He was visibly shaken up. He asked if there was any way that we could meet up for lunch.

We met later that week, but by then the intense emotion had already dissipated. I asked what it was that had so stirred him, and why he had asked to meet up. He said, "I don't know. I guess I really got caught up in the moment. The difference between now and Sunday is like a parable for my life right now. I so badly want to experience spiritual intimacy with God, which is why I was so fired up on Sunday. But then reality sets in, and I can't figure out how to do it, so I revert back to a more detached state."

He went on to share some of his story. He had grown up around church and had fond memories of church, particularly from his high school years. He had a strong "walk with God" during high school, and his recollection was that he felt a nearly constant awareness of the presence of God in his life during this time.

But after high school he headed off for a state university that had quite the reputation for being a party school, and his strong Christian roots were no match. He got sucked into the party culture, and before long God became nothing more than an afterthought. "I wasn't doing anything horrible," he said, "but I was definitely not following God—or even thinking about God, for that matter."

After graduation, Joe moved back to Chicago, where a longing to reconnect with God began to emerge. He lamented that he had let so many years go by without engaging with God.

He visited his parents' church one Sunday, and when the pastor did an altar call for believers to recommit their life to God, Joe immediately responded. He knew it was time to make things right with God and was excited to restart the process of drawing near to God.

Despite multiple attempts at rekindling his spiritual intimacy, however, Joe felt like he was experiencing nothing but failure.

"I am doing all the things I knew to do when I was younger," he said. "All the things that actually seemed to work back then. Read my Bible, have a daily quiet time, go to church on Sundays, get in a small group with some other guys who are trying to grow in their faith. I feel like I get glimpses of God, like I did last Sunday, but they come and go so quickly. I can't seem to find God, and if I do, it feels like he immediately disappears again."

He paused for a moment, and then shared his deepest fear: "I feel like God is punishing me for my waywardness in college. I don't want to believe this is true, but I can't shake the feeling that God is being intentionally evasive. I rejected God in college, and now I think God is rejecting me. Maybe he just wants me to know how it feels."

There it was again—Lie #3 in full effect. Joe was convinced that his mistakes in college had caused God to reject him. As I got to know Joe better, I got to witness just how powerful this lie becomes if it is not combated with truth.

Once the lie gained influence over Joe's perception of God, he began to interpret his entire reality through the lens of that lie. At first it started with just church activities. If Joe was at a prayer meeting, church service, or small group and didn't "feel" anything, he interpreted that as God rejecting him.

Soon it spread to other arenas in his life. Over the course of the next year, Joe got in a car accident, lost a grandparent, and missed out on a promotion that he was really hoping for at work. In all three cases Joe became convinced that God was pouring out punishment for his mistakes during college.

We often have a haunting fear that we are not good enough, well behaved enough, or spiritually informed enough to please God. So we go on a manic and empty search to find the code that will get God to like us again. We become vulnerable to anyone or anything that promises to help us tap into God's good graces, and oftentimes we end up on a wild goose chase for intimacy with God.

Lie #3 tries to convince us that God is distant or evasive or hard to find. It wants us to believe that God has rejected us and that it is now on us to try to find God.

This is the beauty and importance of the Genesis account. Adam and Eve had Paradise but still gave in to sin. Adam and Eve knew the heart of God but still gave in to fear. Adam and Eve knew only God could sustain them yet tried to cover themselves with fig leaves.

But even still, the truth never changed. God never stopped loving them, never stopped pursuing them, never stopped inviting them to walk with him in a spirit of intimacy.

That is why we so badly need to root our understanding of faith in the truth of the Genesis account. God is pursuing you, just as God pursued Adam and Eve. Tenderly, relentlessly, God continues to search for you. God loves you and will never give up on you. No matter what. There is nothing you can do, nothing you can say, nowhere you can run that will stop God from pursuing you.

I had a seminary professor who once claimed that the most important question in the entire Bible comes from Genesis 3:9: "Where are you?"

What the Genesis account reminds us of is that this is never, ever the question *we* need to ask. We never have to wonder if God is there or wonder if God is playing hide-and-seek with us. We never have to wonder if we are able to be in a spiritually intimate relationship with God.

That is because God is always asking the same question. It is the question of love. It is the question of pursuit.

"Where are you?"

////////////

A. W. Tozer writes, "What comes into our minds when we think about God is the most important thing about us."[1] What you believe about the character of God influences every aspect of your life. That is why the lies of the Garden are so heavily focused on distorting God's character.

The Genesis account is not just the source material for Hebrews 11; it is meant to be the platform by which we come to a clear and true understanding of the nature of God.

God is not a vindictive, vengeful being who punishes and rejects to get a point across. It is just the opposite. God's love, mercy, and grace go so far beyond the limits of our imagination that it almost hurts. God pursues us faithfully, tenderly, relentlessly. God invites us to "walk" with him, to experience spiritual intimacy.

This is the center of the faith experience for a follower of Jesus Christ. In John 17 Jesus prays one last time before accepting his mission to die as a ransom for many. In verse 3 he says, "Now this is eternal life: that they know you, the only true God, and Jesus Christ, whom you have sent."

That was his mission—that every person might know God. Jesus lived, died, and was resurrected so that we could experience the transforming power of spiritual intimacy with God.

Let us follow the author, pioneer, and finisher of our faith as he leads us into the most wonderful and life-altering truth known to humankind.

14

//////////////////////

Pleasing God

Any true experience of the Holy gives one the experience of being secretly chosen, invited, and loved. Surely that is why bride and bridegroom, invitations, and wedding banquets are Jesus's most common metaphors for eternal life.

Richard Rohr

Throughout the early stages of my voyage to discover a fuller, more complete picture of faith, one verse I often heard struck at the core of one of my deepest fears:

Without faith it is impossible to please God. (Heb. 11:6)

There was something about that word *impossible* that brought all my latent anxieties to the surface. My fears were triggered each time I saw it, and I would hear a voice of discouragement whisper, "It doesn't actually matter what you do, because you are never going to actually please God. You are never going to have enough faith—it's impossible! So just accept that reality and move on."

That is the problem with fear—it obscures the profound nature of the truth that we so desperately need to embrace. As Richard Rohr says, the unwavering reality is that God "gives one the experience of being secretly chosen, invited, and loved."[1] This is what God desires to give us. God is always near, always ready, always waiting to embrace us.

If it is true that God is relentlessly pursuing spiritual intimacy, and if it is true that some combination of fear, insecurity, and susceptibility to lies is what often thwarts that intimacy, then it really is possible that we can step into the intimate experience God intends for us. It doesn't have to be some overspiritualized ideal; it can and should be the normative, everyday experience for those of us who follow Christ.

We need Jesus to take us to the point of our deepest fears, and we need to trust that he will help us break through those fears, insecurities, and lies, and lead us into "the secret place of the Most High" (Ps. 91:1 NKJV). This is where God gives us that experience of being chosen, invited, and loved. This intimate walking with God is where the deepest parts of our identity are affirmed and strengthened.

When the writer of Hebrews said, "Without faith it is impossible to please God" (11:6), he was intending it to be a source of hope, not discouragement. It is his follow-up commentary to the faith hero Enoch, whose life was exceedingly pleasing to God: "For before he was taken, *he was commended as one who pleased God*" (Heb. 11:5, emphasis added).

I love that phrase! Do you remember how Genesis described the essence of Enoch's life? Do you remember how the greatness of his faith was described? It is rooted in the imagery of the Garden: "Enoch walked faithfully with God" (Gen. 5:24).

Enoch walked faithfully with God, and because of faith in Jesus, I can too.

What the opening account of Genesis shows us—and what the contents of Hebrews 11 confirm—is that the truth of God's love and pursuit never changes. It is not dependent on how well adjusted our behaviors are, how clearly stated our theology is, or how strong our faith appears (to others or to ourselves). God wants to walk with us in spiritual intimacy, and Jesus is shepherding us toward that same reality.

So while we have much to think and reflect on when it comes to spiritual intimacy with God, we also have a freedom that comes from being rooted in a simple and enduring truth: God pursued Adam and Eve in the Garden, and God is pursuing you. Jesus is the Good Shepherd, and at the center of his vision for life is helping you and I to walk with God.

So how do we ensure that the three foundational lies do not get a foothold in our walk with God?

I'd like to share with you a set of antidotes in the form of six questions I ask myself regularly to help me combat the lies of the evil one. You may not phrase the questions exactly as I do, but I'd encourage you to do something similar. Discover ways to stay tethered to the never-changing, life-transforming truth of the invitation to walk with God. Be honest about your fears, and combat the lies. I'm certain that when you do, you will be able to step into the legacy of the great cloud of witnesses who walked with God.

Question 1: Is My Vision Clear?

Dallas Willard was regarded as a modern-day guru of spiritual formation, and he said that all transformation begins with vision.[2] He makes the point that this is true across all disciplines of life. Whether you want to learn a new language, stop smoking, or run a marathon, you will never take meaningful steps without first being emotionally and intellectually connected to the vision. Clear vision becomes especially important for the follower of Christ who longs for deep transformation of the soul.

That is one of the reasons that the image on which the Genesis account hinges is Adam and Eve walking with God. It creates a picture for spiritual intimacy, and that picture is meant to inform a vision so alluring that we would turn over heaven and earth to get it. When our soul comes in contact with this vision, it reminds us that we too are designed to walk with God. It is meant to evoke a sense of nostalgia and longing.

All the men and women of faith listed in Hebrews 11 were flawed and ordinary human beings who became extraordinary people of great faith as they learned to walk with God by faith.

Meditation is one of the most effective practices I use for keeping my vision clear. The opening verses of Psalms emphasize the importance of this: "Blessed is the one . . . whose delight is in the law of the LORD, and who meditates on his law day and night. That person is like a tree planted by streams of water, which yields its fruit in season and whose leaf does not wither" (Ps. 1:1–3).

A tree planted by streams of waters points to strength, stability, depth, longevity, vitality, power, and rootedness. We can't get there without walking with God, and we won't walk with God if we aren't clear on the centrality of this vision in the Christian experience.

That's why I often meditate on the imagery of walking with God from Genesis 3. I ask God to emblazon that truth onto my soul. I ask God to allow it to touch not only my intellect but also my emotions. I ask God to turn that image into a white-hot vision that compels me to move back toward God with courage and expectancy.

Question 2: Am I Listening for God Calling Me?

I've seen time and again how much undo pressure gets added on to the experience of faith when I fall into the trap of assuming that the onus is on me to find God. The moment I begin to believe that I have to initiate a search for God, I have set the stage for lies to alter my spiritual compass.

God did not just initiate and pursue relationship with Adam and Eve in the best times in Paradise—he continued to do so even when they were in the midst of their most broken, alienated state. The pressure was not on Adam and Eve to initiate a reconciliation process with God. God pursued them. God was the one who initiated the search.

We are never the ones who start the search. We are not the ones asking, "Where is God?" God is the one who initiates. God is the one on the search. God is the one who asks the question, "Where are you?" (Gen. 3:9). Even when we find ourselves hungering for and pursuing God, it is still a response to a God who first pursued us.

A woman in our community shared that reflecting on this question became the spiritual breakthrough for her in the journey to move out of feeling "something's missing." She had struggled with a prolonged period of spiritual stagnation and was beginning to give in to the fear that God was intentionally being elusive. But when she came to understand the magnitude of the question, "Where are you?" everything began to change. She said that from that point forward, each time she would start to wonder if God had abandoned her, she would say this prayer: *God, I know you are present right now, and I trust that you are trying to reveal yourself to me. Maybe it's my sin that's in the way—if so, I confess and repent right now. Maybe it's my doubt. Maybe it's my fear. But whatever it is, I know you are here, and I know you are pursuing me. Help me to live in that truth.*

I find the same dynamic often is present in my own walk with God. In order to combat my fears, my doubts, and the strength of the lies, I need to consistently remember both the vision and the question that God uses to initiate spiritual intimacy: *Where are you?*

Question 3: Am I Earnestly Seeking God?

It might appear paradoxical to reflect on the question, "Am I earnestly seeking God?" immediately after emphasizing the fact that God is the one who initiates the search. But that paradox is the heart of Hebrews 11. Earlier in the book the writer of Hebrews emphasizes that when we "hold firmly to the faith" (4:14), we develop the boldness to step confidently into the presence of God. This is the same thing he is saying in Hebrews 11:6:

> Without faith it is impossible to please God, because anyone who comes to him must believe that he exists and that he rewards those who earnestly seek him.

When he says, "anyone who comes to him must believe," he is rooting that belief in the timeless truth of God's pursuit. Once we come to the firm conviction that God is on the search for us, the stage is set to fully embrace the spiritual longings we so desperately feel. Now we can "earnestly seek him," because we know he is already earnestly seeking us.

When I meditate on this question, my goal is to make an honest assessment of the degree to which I am actively responding to the pursuit of God. Walking with God is an activity that requires both parties to invest, and I think that is why the writer of Hebrews emphasizes this point. If I just sit back passively and wait to be zapped by intimacy, it is unlikely that I am going to experience the dynamic relationship that I am so genuinely craving.

God is pursuing, but an active response from us is also required. If we trust that God already longs for spiritual intimacy and that God is already on the search for us, then chasing that vision with full conviction seems to be the most natural response in the world.

Question 4: Am I Aware of My Fears and Insecurities?

I have talked about the role of fear throughout the book, so I won't elaborate much here. I believe that fear is the primary inhibitor to every dimension of great faith. It was fear that impaired the ability of Adam and Eve to respond to God's pursuit: "I heard you in the garden, and I was *afraid* because I was naked; so I hid" (Gen. 3:10, emphasis added).

In meditating on this question, I revisit the core, macro fears that have been part of my lifelong journey and honestly acknowledge the degree to which they continue to have an effect on me (as I said in chapter 9, naming our "boat" is one of the most important activities that we can engage in). I also look for the smaller, more prevalent ways that fear or insecurity is preventing me from fully embracing the vision of spiritual intimacy.

Question 5: Am I Conscious of the Impact of the Lies in My Life?

I have always found it significant that Jesus refers to Satan by the moniker "father of lies" (John 8:44). As C. S. Lewis says, it is important to avoid either extreme when thinking about the "thief." It is a mistake to overstate his power, but it is also a mistake to underestimate his influence.

I have found that the easiest way to find a healthy balance between the two extremes is by thinking of the evil one primarily as a liar. In the same way that the serpent wreaked havoc in the Garden by distorting God's truth, so the thief is looking for ways to do the same in our lives.

Therefore I regularly go through the three lies seen in the Genesis account, and I specifically apply each of those three lies to my current spiritual reality. I ask myself four sub-questions to get a quick pulse:

1. In what ways am I disregarding or disobeying the commands of God in my life?
2. In what ways am I calling into question the goodness of God?
3. In what ways am I pursuing a sense of meaning and identity outside of God?
4. In what ways have I bought into the lie that God has either rejected me or that God is for some reason evading my requests?

Answering these questions enables me to monitor the degree to which the three lies are distorting my vision of God's character. When I am conscious of the ways the lies are impacting me, I can then begin to partner with God to turn my gaze away from the lies and instead "fix my eyes" upon Jesus.

Question 6: Am I "Fixing My Eyes" upon Jesus?

Hebrews 12:2 offers the defining image of this book. The author of Hebrews says that in order to be led into great faith, we must fix our eyes on Jesus, who is the author, pioneer, and finisher of our faith.

The significance of those three words—author, pioneer, and finisher—never seems to fade for me. The invitation to walk with God is directly tied to my vision of Jesus, and I therefore go back over the implications of all three of those words on a regular basis.

When considering whether I am "fixing my eyes on Jesus," I often look to Luke 24:13–35 to serve as a template for what that practically looks like. This "Emmaus Road" story is one of the only accounts I know of in the Bible where we get a real-time look at Jesus acting as the author, pioneer, and finisher of faith, and I have found it helpful for my own understanding.

In this passage Luke tells us that there are two men walking down the road to Emmaus, and they are struggling to make sense of the crucifixion of Jesus Christ. The resurrected Jesus joins their conversation, though he is not immediately recognized.

Once Jesus deemed the time was right, he began to help them clear up the confusion they were feeling. "And beginning with Moses and all the Prophets, he explained to them what was said in all the Scriptures concerning himself" (v. 27).

This verse is a powerful reminder to me that everything in the Bible is ultimately pointing to the risen, resurrected Jesus. The Genesis account, the Pentateuch, the Prophets, the Epistles—it all culminates in him.

This is one of the reasons to go deeper in our knowledge of Scripture. The apostle Paul says that faith comes from hearing, and that hearing comes from the Word of God (see Rom. 10:17). As Scripture becomes more and more part of who I am, it helps me to understand Jesus better and deepens my capacity to fix my eyes on him in faith.

The encounter between Jesus and the two men finishes like this:

> As they approached the village to which they were going, Jesus continued on as if he were going farther. But they urged him strongly, "Stay with us, for it is nearly evening; the day is almost over." So he went in to stay with them.
>
> When he was at the table with them, he took bread, gave thanks, broke it and began to give it to them. Then their eyes were opened and they recognized him, and he disappeared from their sight. They asked each other, "Were not our hearts burning within us while he talked with us on the road and opened the Scriptures to us?" (Luke 24:28–32)

What can we take from this?

First, Jesus initiates this encounter by entering into their conversation, but then he waits for them to reciprocate before taking it any further. They beg Jesus to "stay with us" (v. 29). It's important to recognize how Jesus is already pursuing us and then to follow that up by telling Jesus how badly we want his continued leadership and guidance in our lives.

Second, this story shows again how intimate faith is intended to be. Jesus does not appear to them as a removed deity or as an abstract ideal. He sat at a table and shared a meal with them, and it was within this intimate exchange that they experienced spiritual revelation. Jesus really is risen and resurrected, and we really are attached to him by faith.

Third and finally, this encounter gives us language to understand what it means to hear the voice of Jesus. I have referred throughout to John 10 and Jesus's insistence that the sheep know the voice of the shepherd. But even when we take that promise at face value, it can be confusing at times to know exactly *how* to recognize the voice of Jesus.

The most consistent way I have learned to recognize the voice of Jesus in my life is by applying the imagery from Luke 24:32: "Were not our hearts burning within us while he talked with us on the road and opened the Scriptures to us?"

Do you have moments when you are thinking about God or reading Scripture and your heart begins to "burn"? It's a hard thing to describe to another person, and yet it is as real as a hunger pang or a strong emotion.

One of the mistakes I made as a younger Christian was to pay too little attention to those moments when my heart "burned." I spent too much time looking for unmistakable, dramatic interventions of God in my life (which I have only experienced a handful of times) and too little time looking for the subtle but real moments when my heart was burning.

This passage helped me to realize that Jesus was speaking to me much more frequently than I initially thought. Sometimes the "burn" would come in the midst of a conversation, and a phrase would stick in my mind for the rest of the day. Sometimes the burn would come from an idea stimulated by listening to music or going for a run. Oftentimes it would happen through a sermon I was listening to or a passage of Scripture I was reading.

But I still didn't take it far enough. Recognizing those moments is one thing, but translating them into opportunities for spiritual intimacy is another. I was doing the first; I was recognizing with greater frequency that Jesus was moving in my life. But I wasn't doing the second; whatever event was next up in my schedule would distract me, and the potency of what had happened slowly began to dissipate. Within a day or two I wouldn't even remember the burning moment I had with God.

Some of the best strides I've made in my ability to walk intimately with God have come from marrying the revelations I'm given by God with the choice to engage him in that very moment. I must fuse those two together—recognizing the moments of my heart burning and then saturating myself in those moments through meditation.

Now whenever I sense my heart burning, I treat it as a spiritually sacred moment. Even if it is a slight burn, I choose to interpret it as an invitation from God. From a practical standpoint, I have learned that it's important for me to record both the cause of the burn and the content of the burn right away, with the intent of meditating on it later in the day. Sometimes that means scribbling it down on a random scrap of paper. Often it means recording it into my iPhone (I like this, because I can pretend I'm talking on my phone while actually creating an audio file for myself of what just happened).

I try to create space later that same day to take a walk and to meditate on that which made my heart burn. I treat the whole thing as a Jesus-sparked encounter, designed for the purpose of spiritual intimacy. I ask Jesus to guide me into deeper truth about whatever the idea or topic was. I ask him to help me understand what this particular word might mean. I ask him to reveal more of God to me through the meditation and to take me deeper into the secret place of the Most High.

At the end of the day, it's always about being deeply connected to the everlasting, never-changing truth about God. God is on the search for us, pursuing us to experience spiritual intimacy. Jesus is trying to lead us past our fears, through the lies, and into this very reality.

What happened to the two men on the road to Emmaus is exactly what Jesus wants to happen to us: "Then their eyes were opened and they recognized him" (Luke 24:31).

May this be the consistent reality for you as you follow Jesus in faith. May your eyes be opened, and may you recognize the One who is love itself.

Part 4

FAITH
AND
MISSION

15

///////////////////////

Mission Impossible

Our task as image-bearing, God-loving, Christ-shaped, Spirit-filled Christians, following Christ and shaping our world, is to announce redemption to a world that has discovered its fallenness, to announce healing to a world that has discovered its brokenness, to proclaim love and trust to a world that knows only exploitation, fear and suspicion.

N. T. Wright

Joshua 1 records the contents of the spiritual conversation between Joshua and God. God's message to Joshua brings together all three dimensions of faith:

> As I was with Moses, so I will be with you; I will never leave you nor forsake you. Be strong and courageous, because you will lead these people to inherit the land I swore to their ancestors to give them. (Josh. 1:5–6)

God tells Joshua to be "strong and courageous" (v. 6)—Joshua is going to need an elevated faith experience to overcome the fear he is facing. God also tells Joshua that just as he was with Moses, "so

I will be with you" (v. 5)—Joshua is being invited into an intimate, interactive relationship with God.

Then God used the word "because" to bind it all together. God says, "Be strong and courageous, *because* . . ." (v. 6).

What was on the other side of *because*?

Because . . . God had a *mission* for Joshua. The end result of this faith encounter was a call to participate in a mission that was close to the heart of God.

What comes to your mind when you hear the word *mission*?

When I was young, I was part of a church that sponsored families involved with global missions. If you felt a call to relocate to a foreign country for the purpose of evangelizing unreached people groups, our church was excited to support that. To demonstrate its commitment to missions, the church placed a large bulletin board filled with pictures of missionaries representing dozens of countries on a prominent wall in the foyer.

It was inspiring to see families who took "mission" so seriously, and I assumed that this was its meaning. Mission represented people who were willing to sacrifice everything in the name of Christ to move to a foreign location.

That narrow definition of mission no longer seemed to apply once I entered the business world. Spiegel, my first employer, also used the word *mission*, but the company certainly was not describing Christian workers doing cross-cultural work in foreign countries.

At Spiegel headquarters, the first thing you saw was a large silver sign broadcasting their "mission statement" in bright red letters. I don't remember the exact wording of their mission statement, but it revolved around some combination of customer service, earning profits, and giving back to the community.

I spent the next seven years in corporate America and saw lots of mission statements. It was very faddish for companies to spend lots of time and energy constructing the perfect one. Soon I no longer thought of "mission" as having anything to do with church—I now thought of it solely as a business word used to describe a company's vision and anticipated outcomes.

That was also around the time when the old television series *Mission Impossible* was given a modern facelift and turned into a movie franchise with Tom Cruise. Each episode (and movie) would begin with a secret government agent receiving his instructions on a tape, CD, or iPhone. The device would then self-destruct as the unforgettable theme music blared in the background. In these movies, "mission" had nothing to do with church or business. Instead, it was describing a high-stakes assignment being given to a top secret agent.

So which was it? Was mission something Christians did when they signed up for daring overseas adventures? Was mission something companies did while providing goods and services? Was mission something top secret government agents were assigned to accomplish? And did any of this matter to the average, everyday Christian like me?

The answer came to me in an unexpected place and from an unexpected person. His name was Thad, and I will be forever a different person because of the simple yet profound ways in which he lived out mission.

I was twenty-two when I first visited Axis, the twentysomethings ministry at Willow Creek Community Church. I didn't know what to expect, and I was pleasantly surprised by my experience. There were more Christian young adults in one room than I had met collectively in my whole life. There was relevant music, a clever presentation, and an edgy and inviting atmosphere.

However, when the service ended and the lights came back on, I suddenly became very self-conscious. I didn't know a single person at Axis, and I wasn't sure what the protocol was for someone who was visiting for the first time.

It was a surreal feeling. I had grown up in church all my life, yet now I was completely out of my element. I was eager to meet people yet wasn't sure how to begin. I wanted to get connected yet didn't know what to do next.

I slowly stood up and awkwardly lingered by my seat, certain that someone would eventually notice me. I was hoping that maybe one of the leaders of the ministry would come and say hi, and then I could follow him around and figure out what I was supposed to do next.

But no leader, or anyone else for that matter, came to say hi. I stood there for as long as I could, but I felt like the entire room was staring at me, wondering why I was there by myself.

Trying to summon a final burst of courage, I headed to the back of the room. I lingered again, hoping that my presence would send out some type of homing beacon shouting, "Say hello to me!" The back of the room gave me a better view of the gym, and I looked around to see what everyone was doing. It seemed every person there knew each other, and it became apparent that I simply wasn't being noticed. I was discouraged and headed out the back door, thinking I might not ever come back.

The next week I decided I should try again. Something had stirred inside of me when I was at Axis the week before, and I wanted to see if it would happen again. I disliked that feeling of standing around awkwardly at the end but hoped that would be a onetime experience.

Unfortunately, the second visit was nearly identical. I was again amazed at the number of twentysomethings who attended, I was again inspired by the service, and I was still eager to get more involved. But when the service ended, I was immediately filled with that same sense of social unease that had marked my previous experience. In fact, this time it seemed to be even more exaggerated. It was my second time, and I felt like I was supposed to know the rules, but it seemed less clear than ever how to get involved.

I did the entire routine again. I slowly gathered up my stuff, giving as much of an opportunity as possible for those nearby to say hello. I walked awkwardly to the back of the room and stood there for what felt like an eternity. I pretended I was looking for somebody, hoping that the mystery person would buy me enough time to find something else to do. When it became clear that I was going to be unsuccessful again, I bailed, feeling frustrated once again.

When the following week rolled around, I had very mixed feelings. On the one hand, I wasn't sure I belonged and didn't really feel like going through the after-service theatrics again. On the other hand, something had been stirred in me each of the first two times. I figured I would give it one more try. This would be the make-or-break night. Either I would meet some people and get connected, or I would not come back.

Everything about my third time at Axis seemed to be pointing to a futile and final experience. I still liked the vibe, but my inability to meet anyone there was becoming too frustrating. It seemed that everyone there knew each other already, and it didn't matter how long I lingered afterward. I felt like I was starting my first day at a new school all over again. I didn't care how great this service was; it simply wasn't worth this level of anxiety. I arrived at the regrettable conclusion that this place was not for me and headed toward the door.

I was less than ten feet from the exit when I felt someone grab my shoulder from behind. I turned around to discover a gregarious, outgoing guy with a giant smile. He said, "Hi, my name is Thad. I haven't met you yet. Are you new here?"

Finally! It had seemed an eternity and I was just about to quit, but now I had finally met someone at Axis. Thad asked me a bunch of get-to-know-you questions, and with each one I began to feel more at ease. He seemed in no rush to move on. He began to tell me more about Axis. He was one of the leaders in the ministry, and it was clear he was very passionate about it.

When it seemed that the interaction was heading toward its conclusion, I began to get nervous. Thad was my only connection to Axis, and I feared that if I couldn't think of a way to keep the conversation going, I would lose my only in.

Once again Thad took the initiative and helped me figure out what to do next with a simple invitation: "Hey, we are all heading over to a restaurant down the street. Do you have plans? Why don't you come join us? You can follow me over if you want."

It's amazing how such simple words can be so life-giving. This seemingly small invitation transported me from quivering with fear to now feeling a sense of confidence well up within me. Someone cared. I mattered. Now I could open myself up to more fully experience what God was doing.

I met a dozen new people that night, and by the time the night was over I had agreed to visit the small group that most of them were part of. Soon after that I joined their group, and the experience of working out faith in the context of community gave me a new vision of God as the central force in my life. I began to think about God and faith all the time, and I became a high-octane volunteer at Axis. The more involved I got, the more great people I met, and the more I could feel myself changing. It was all happening so fast, and I loved it.

A few months into this rapid growth process, it dawned on me that none of this would be happening if it weren't for Thad. I began to have flashbacks of the feelings of isolation I had experienced after my first two visits to Axis. I remembered the vow I made that if I didn't meet someone on my third try, I wouldn't return. Everything had changed for me that night, and it was all due to Thad introducing himself to me.

It also struck me that it was quite a risk on Thad's part, and I suddenly became really curious as to what possessed him to do that. Why did he feel the need to track me down and say hello before I left? What caused him to take such a big relational risk? So I asked Thad if we could have lunch that week.

When we sat down, I started by telling him how much it meant that he had reached out. I told him that I had experienced a huge degree of life change since I started coming to Axis, and I apologized that it had taken me so long to realize that it was his risk to say hello that set all of the pieces in motion.

He was gracious and unassuming, as I expected he would be, downplaying his role. I then asked if he would share with me why he had chased me down like that.

After pausing, he finally replied, "Well, if you want to know the truth, it's because God sent me to go get you."

God had *sent* him? In my Pentecostal upbringing, I used to hear language like that all the time, but I had not heard something like that even once at Willow. And it certainly didn't sound like something Thad would usually say. I asked him to elaborate, and he told me his story:

> I used to just come to the Axis service to connect with my friends and have an experience with God and maybe learn something. Those things weren't bad, but it was all about me. Then I heard a sermon that really convicted me. The pastor used the words from Isaiah 6 when God asks, "Whom shall I send?" He told us that this is what "mission" sounds like—God is always asking "Whom shall I send?" He told us that if a Christ follower will listen for that question, their life will be forever changed.
>
> I was moved by the sermon, and I went and talked to the pastor afterward. I asked him how I could practically implement that into my everyday life. He said, "Every time you enter into an environment, you

make a choice. Will you enter into that environment with a me-first attitude or a mission-first attitude? If you enter with the first, you will not hear the voice of God. But if you enter with the second, you will hear God asking the question of mission."

That was right when Axis was starting, and I decided that I would change my attitude when I came to Axis. Instead of coming on Saturday night with a me-first attitude, I was going to start coming with a mission-first attitude.

The night you came was the first time I tried that. I came to Axis and prayed, "God, if you are asking whom to send, I am volunteering! If there is someone who is disconnected, or alienated from church, or on the margins of our community, show them to me."

But then just as quickly as I prayed it, I got sucked back into my normal attitude. When the service ended I was just talking with my friends and having a good time. But then the weirdest thing happened. I saw you walking toward the exit, and I swear I heard God say, "Him—that is the one. Go get him!" All I could think was, "Really? He's leaving. Can't you send me toward someone else?" But God stirred my heart. I felt that if I didn't run over there and grab you, I would be disobeying God. So I said, "All right, here goes . . ." I guess the rest is history.

It would be hard for me to fully describe how moved I was by that conversation. I was filled with so many emotions all at once. I felt thankful that Thad had been listening to the voice of God and grateful that he had the courage to follow through on what he sensed God leading him to do.

I also felt overwhelmed by the grace and goodness of God. I had always believed that God loved me in a general way, the same way that God is supposed to love all people. But I had never really felt that love in a personalized way.

Now here was Thad telling me the story of how God sent him to come get me. I remembered what a fragile place I was in spiritually, and I wondered what would have happened if Thad had not greeted me that night. The fact that God saw my fragile condition and then sent someone to come get me was overwhelming to me. It was one of the most concrete ways I have ever felt the love of God.

I basked in the glow of this reality for a few days. It was truly remarkable that God had loved me enough to send Thad to go and get me. Soon thereafter, another important detail of Thad's story began to emerge.

I started to think about the language that Thad used to describe his attitude when he came to Axis. He was consciously trying to shift out of a "me-first" attitude and into a "mission-first" attitude. I had heard mission defined in so many different ways—overseas missionaries, corporate mission statements, Hollywood spy missions—but the way Thad was using it now was unfamiliar. He was taking it out of the abstract, untouchable realm and was making it a concrete reality that he could align his attitude with.

It had never occurred to me that mission was something I could participate in. I had the same combination of insecurity and ignorance that many of us do—I thought Christian mission was for a small group of special people, made to make a stadium-sized impact to count, and required a level of faith that I could only dream of. It certainly wasn't for someone as unspectacular as myself.

Yet being sent on mission was exactly how Thad thought of himself. Thad viewed each Saturday night service as a high-stakes, God-led mission. He entered into that environment prayerful and ready, knowing that his responsiveness could change the course of someone's life.

At that point I began to experience a strange sensation. I thought, *If Thad can be used on a mission by God, maybe I can be used by God too*. Thad took mission seriously, and as a result my life had been transformed. Was it possible that I could play that same kind of role for someone else?

I decided to get out my Bible and study Isaiah 6, the same passage that instilled a sense of mission into Thad. There Isaiah describes the most powerful and formative encounter he ever had with God. It shaped the direction of his life and created a template for how he would move forward in faith. His encounter followed the same biblical pattern of fear and faith, faith and intimacy, and faith and mission as discussed throughout this book.

Isaiah's vision began with seeing God seated on a throne, and above God were angels singing, "Holy, holy, holy is the LORD Almighty; the whole earth is full of his glory" (v. 3).

Isaiah's initial response to the glory of God was fear: "'Woe to me!' I cried. 'I am ruined! For I am a man of unclean lips, and I live among a people of unclean lips, and my eyes have seen the King, the LORD Almighty'" (v. 5).

God responded to Isaiah in a warm, gentle, and intimate way. "Then one of the seraphim flew to me with a live coal in his hand, which he had taken with tongs from the altar. With it he touched my mouth and said, 'See, this has touched your lips; your guilt is taken away and your sin atoned for'" (vv. 6–7).

The message of forgiveness was brought powerfully to Isaiah. He realized that by grace his guilt had been taken away and his sins atoned for. He would never again have to wonder if his bad deeds or impure thoughts would separate him from the love of God. He had been redeemed, and God was inviting him to drink deeply of this grace and mercy.

After experiencing this intimate touch from God, Isaiah then shifted into the space defined by faith and mission: "Then I heard the voice of the Lord saying, 'Whom shall I send? And who will go for us?'" (v. 8).

This is the starting point of the Christian understanding of mission. God looks at the world and asks this pair of questions: "Whom shall I send?" and "Who will go for us?"

That was the set of questions that transformed Isaiah's life. It was also the set of questions that had transformed Thad's life. By entering into environments like Axis with an attentive ear to the voice of God, he was able to align his actions with the missional question of God: "Whom shall I send?"

As I read the account of Isaiah, I felt empowered. If being on mission meant I had to become Billy Graham, I knew I couldn't do it. But if being on mission meant simply aligning myself to listen and respond to God's questions of "Whom shall I send? Who will go for us?" then I felt confident I could very well do this.

Before attending the next Axis, I prayed, "God, I've never even thought about mission before. Everything I do is for myself. Even going to church is for me. But tonight, I ask that you would help me to shift from a me-first attitude to a mission-first attitude. I will listen for your voice. And if you would be so willing, please guide me into the next steps of mission." And with that I was off.

Arriving at Axis that night, I felt like the experience had taken on a whole new meaning. It was one thing to go with the intent of seeing some friends and hanging out afterward. It was something entirely different to go with the intent of being ready for mission. When I imagined being sent to a person in the same way that Thad had been sent to come get me, the night seemed to have an incredible sense of meaning and purpose.

When the service ended I began praying the words of Isaiah 6. I imagined God asking, "Whom shall I send?" and prayed in a quiet voice, "Here am I. Send me!" It initially felt foreign, but it was also exciting. I had been coming to Axis for a few months now, but I couldn't remember ever praying as much as I was on this night.

I also became conscious of how much fear was rushing through my body. I had felt some level of anxiety the first time I came to Axis, but that fear seemed so trivial compared to this. Before I had feared that I wouldn't meet anybody. Now I feared that I would mess up the mission of God! Doubts and excuses began to flood my mind like fast-growing weeds:

"You haven't been around Axis that long—what gives you the right to suddenly become an authority?"

"You've only been following Jesus for a few months, and you don't even know what you are talking about. You should leave this for those who are more spiritually mature."

"What if you get asked a question you don't know the answer to? You will look like a fool, and they would have been better off talking to someone else."

I was so self-conscious at that point of my life, and I rarely took relational risks. Now here I was intentionally seeking out disconnected newcomers, and it filled me with anxiety. But each time I would feel nervous, I would remember the night Thad listened to God and came to find me. What if he had given in to fear? What if he had lost heart? This gave me the courage to push past my boundary of comfort and to seek the person that God might be sending me to reach.

I didn't hear any audible voice sending me missional directives. I didn't see a glowing halo over the person I was supposed to meet. I simply wandered around the room looking for someone who had the same expression I'd had when I was visiting.

As I scanned the room, I saw two people lingering near the exit, and they had the telltale signs of being new. They looked nervous and uncertain of the post-service ritual. They appeared to want to meet someone, but it seemed obvious they wouldn't last long.

Once again fear arose. Should I go over there? What if I introduced myself and found out that they were Axis regulars? I would feel so stupid.

As I struggled to reconcile my own fear, I looked around the room. As I did, I could see what they saw. It looked the same as it had looked to me a few months earlier. When the service ended, the people who were already connected found their friends to greet and catch up with. Those who were not connected left almost immediately. I knew how intimidating the picture must appear to these two. I worked up my courage and went over and introduced myself.

My hunch had been correct. They were brand-new visitors, and they didn't know anyone at Axis. They were within seconds of leaving because it appeared that everyone else already knew each other. I didn't know what to do next, so I just followed Thad's protocol. I told them that we would all be going out to a restaurant after Axis and asked if they would like to come. I told them they could follow me over and that I would make some introductions. They happily accepted.

As we drove over to the restaurant, I was hit with the realization that I had stepped into a space with God that I had never anticipated, and I felt overwhelmed with gratitude. It was like nothing I had experienced up to that point. I wasn't sure what would happen next for these two. I had no idea if the connections they made on this Saturday night would blossom into great friendships the way they did my first night.

Though I was unsure of what this night would represent for them, I was very clear on what it represented for me. I had just participated in my first Christian mission. I had listened for the question, "Whom shall I send?" and I answered, "Here am I. Send me!" I had almost faltered because of fear and self-consciousness, but I came through. I did my best to be positioned and postured to hear from God, and I did my best to find the person I had been sent to get that night.

When I trace back through the story of my life, I see clearly that one of the key turning points in moving into an experience of abundant life was when I discovered this word *mission*. What began as a mindset shift at the Saturday night Axis service evolved into a new way of interacting with every arena of my life.

If God could use me to participate in mission at Axis, then why not be missional when I was at work? What about social settings—was God on mission there too? What about the huge problems of society? God had to care about those, right? A whole new dimension of faith was beginning to open up to me, and it was incredibly revitalizing.

It was as if God was whispering in my ear, "Daniel, open up your eyes to see not only what I am doing in your life but what I am doing all around you. Will you rise up and volunteer when I ask, 'Whom shall I send?'" I said yes that day, and I am still saying yes today. So many of us are silently wondering, "What is missing from my relationship with God?" Saying yes to God's mission may be the life-changing answer to that very question.

16

//////////////

Lord of the Harvest

Jesus takes us always step by step. He doesn't reveal the whole all
at once. So I would tell anyone who feels this: Please take another
step and do something to the closest person—inside your family,
inside your town, inside your church. You can encourage someone
with a word. You can give a flower to someone. You can do something.
When you do, Jesus will open the door for you for more.

Mama Maggie Gobran

The word *mission* is slowly making its way back into church vocabulary, and I think that is both good and bad. It's good, because *mission*
is a really important word. It's bad because hardly anyone knows what
it means, yet it constantly gets thrown around anyway.

I smile each time a visitor at River City asks me if we are a "missional" church, because I wonder if they themselves know what they
are asking. I asked a recent guest what he was asking exactly with
that question, and his answer was refreshingly honest: "I don't really
know. My best friend from college said he goes to a missional church,
so I figured I should ask. I think it has to do with the style of music
and whether or not you burn candles, but if I'm honest, I have no
idea what I'm actually asking."

I appreciate the renewed interest in the word, but I fear it could just turn into another cliché that comes and goes. So what does it mean to be missional?

Once you have the right lens to look through, you discover that the theme of mission saturates the entire Bible. One of the classic texts for gaining a comprehensive understanding of mission is Luke 10, and this is the passage that has most influenced my understanding of mission.

The context of this chapter is just as important as the contents. Luke was a doctor, and he took a very logic-oriented approach to his accounting of the life and ministry of Jesus Christ. When he wrote the Gospel of Luke, he used the first nine chapters to essentially ask a single question: "Who is Jesus?" Luke explores the teachings, the claims, the miracles, and the debates, and he invites the reader to ask that question with him.

Luke uses the confession of Peter to resolve this question in chapter 9. Jesus asks the disciples who the crowds say he is, and their answers vary from John the Baptist to Elijah. Jesus then says, "What about you? Who do you say I am?" Peter boldly declares, "God's Messiah" (v. 20). This answer represents Luke's resolution as well. Jesus is not just a great teacher or even a prophet—he is the Messiah, the one sent from God for whom the Hebrews had been waiting a thousand years.

With the resolution now made that Jesus is the Messiah, the topic shifts to discipleship. Chapter 10 launches into a new question: What does it mean to be a disciple of Jesus Christ?

Jesus now moves beyond the original twelve disciples that he had already been training and mentoring. He establishes an additional seventy-two disciples to train them in his way. They represent the first generation of Christ followers, and the first topic to be covered in their training is mission. Jesus begins here:

> After this the Lord appointed seventy-two others and sent them two by two ahead of him to every town and place where he was about to go. He told them, "The harvest is plentiful, but the workers are few. Ask the Lord of the harvest, therefore, to send out workers into his harvest field." (Luke 10:1–2)

Within those two verses is some of the most comprehensive theology on mission in the whole Bible. Jesus establishes three foundations that undergird mission, and this became the basis upon which they participated with Jesus in his ministry.

It has always struck me as an interesting detail that the most extensive explanation of mission is saved for the seventy-two. These seventy-two Christ followers represent every person who is serious about following Jesus—every person who considers himself or herself a disciple of Jesus. If we follow Jesus by faith, then we follow him into mission.

Once a Christ follower grasps the three foundations that Jesus gives to the seventy-two, mission becomes a whole new and exciting frontier. Spiritual growth, elevated faith, fullness of life—these can't happen in the ways we long for without mission.

Foundation 1: Mission Is an Extension of God's Love Story

> The harvest is plentiful, but the workers are few. Ask the Lord of the harvest, therefore, to send out workers into his harvest field.
>
> Luke 10:2

Many names are used to describe God in the Bible, but one of my personal favorites is "Lord of the harvest." When Jesus sent the seventy-two disciples on their first mission, the image he chose to root mission in was the metaphor of an abundant harvest.

Most of us don't live in a climate or culture where we are personally involved with the reaping of a plentiful harvest, so it's easy to miss the significance of this metaphor. Jesus was speaking to first-century Palestinians living in an agrarian economy, and the fact that they were so dependent on agriculture as their primary means for support and sustenance made this image strike home.

In a culture like theirs, life revolved around the harvest. Whether the harvest was marked by abundance or deficit was literally a life-or-death issue. If the harvest came in under expectations, the entire economy would be vulnerable. But if the harvest was abundant, as Jesus describes here, then the entire town could look expectantly toward a prosperous and healthy year.

What I love so much about this metaphor is that it is used to describe not only mission but the very essence and character of God.

Does the description of God as "Lord of the harvest" match your honest view of God?

It didn't match mine, at least not my view growing up. Instead of seeing God as "Lord of the harvest," I saw God more like a scene from a documentary that I recently watched. It was exploring a war-torn region in the Middle East, and it was focused on the desperation of the locals who were left to pick up the pieces after the conflict.

One of the scenes showed a line of families that extended around the entire perimeter of an aid camp. The camera zoomed in on one particular UN worker whose job it was to distribute food to each of the families. The level of supplies was not nearly enough for the demand, and the UN worker had no choice but to put significant rations on the food in hopes of stretching it out further. This didn't stop each successive family from begging him to make an exception, and he had the unenviable task of explaining to them that the shortage was too significant for him to exceed the preset limit.

As I watched this with a spirit of sadness, I realized that this was also the picture of God I carried for many years. I thought of God's love as something that was in short supply, something that had to be almost pried out of his hands. I imagined myself as one of those individuals in a long line of desperate people, and I thought of God as the UN worker who could give out only a fraction of what each of us was asking for.

I'm not sure how this view first formed, but it is diametrically opposed to how God is described in Luke 10. My view of God was marked by deficit and lack; the view Jesus gives is marked by abundance and prosperity.

This is one of those texts that has been very healing for my broken image of God. It helped cement for me the truth that God does not need to be cajoled or convinced to give freely of his love. It's exactly the opposite—God's love is compared to a plentiful harvest. That summons a mental picture of a barn that is so abundant from the harvest that it is practically exploding at the seams.

Does your view of God sync up with the description that Jesus uses? Do the mission of love and the attitude of abundance match your experience of God?

I hope so. And if they don't currently, I hope they will over time. It can be a challenge to serve an unseen God in a world filled with brokenness and suffering, and we can easily be weighed down with feelings of desperation rather than lifted up with the reality of God's goodness. Part of this goodness has to do with the abundance of his presence that he offers not only to us but to the entire world. Seeing him accurately in the face of a world clouded with hardship is vital for your own relationship with God and also important for your ability to participate in mission.

God's primary motivation for mission is love, and that must be the starting point for how we engage it. Isn't that exactly what the most famous verse on mission in the Bible tells us? "For God so loved the world that he gave his one and only Son" (John 3:16).

Mission is fundamentally a love story. It is the story of a God who loves his whole creation and particularly loves his prized creation, human beings. It is the story of a God who sees the damage that has been caused by sin and selfishness and who is motivated to save us from that which has gone awry. It is the story of a God who redeems and renews, who reconciles and restores. Biblical mission is a love story.

This truth is seen right from the opening accounts of the Bible. Do you remember the Garden account and the question that is at the center of the story? In Genesis 3, after Adam and Eve sinned, God comes looking for them and asks, "Where are you?" (v. 9).

Through this question the abundance of God's love is so clearly seen. It is Adam and Eve's opportunity to see that despite their brokenness and sin, God will never stop loving them, never stop pursuing them, and never stop inviting them to walk intimately with him.

Through this question the first foundation of mission is also clearly seen. Before God ever "sends" someone on mission, God goes on mission himself. This pattern is then repeated throughout the Bible. God the Father sends Jesus into mission; the Father and Jesus send the Holy Spirit into mission; and finally, the entire Godhead sends us into mission.

As the story unfolds, the source and motivation remain the same. Mission begins in the heart of God and is motivated by love.

Foundation 2: God Sends Us into Mission

After this the Lord appointed seventy-two others and sent them two by two ahead of him to every town and place where he was about to go. He told them, "The harvest is plentiful, but the workers are few. Ask the Lord of the harvest, therefore, to send out workers into his harvest field. Go! I am sending you out like lambs among wolves."

Luke 10:1–3

The word *mission* is used multiple times in this text, though you won't see it in the English version. Our English word *mission* actually comes from the Latin word *missio*, which translates into English as "sent." Though the Bible was originally written in Hebrew (Old Testament) and Greek/Aramaic (New Testament), Latin was the language by which people interacted with Scripture for over 1,200 years (to give a sense of historical proportion, English translations of the Bible didn't appear until almost AD 1600).

Because Latin was the language in which people learned the concepts of Scripture for so long, it informed many of the English words we use today to describe rich theological terms. *Mission* is one of those.

Once we realize that *mission* is simply the Latin word for *sent*, our eyes can be opened to the constancy of mission in the Bible. In this text alone we see it three times. Jesus "sent" the disciples out two by two (v. 1). Jesus tells them to pray that God would "send" more workers into the harvest (v. 2). Jesus tells them that he is "sending" them out like lambs among wolves (v. 3). The language of mission saturates the entire account.

Here is where the first two foundations begin to converge. The first foundation is that mission begins in the heart of God. Mission is a love story—it is God renewing and restoring the world that he loves. The second foundation is that God "sends" us into that mission.

When those two intersect, we come face-to-face with the strategy of God—a strategy that has always struck me as quite bewildering. God sends *us* to declare and to demonstrate that love to the world. God's one and only plan for making this love known in concrete ways rests on Christ followers who take seriously the call of mission.

Crazy, right?

If I were God's public relations consultant, I would tell God that this seems like an ineffective strategy. Even on our best days, human beings seem to be quite limited in our ability to reflect the goodness and love of God. At our worst, we make God's love seem trivial, relegated to a small number of hot-button issues, and at times we even make it appear impotent. Why would God build his outreach strategy around sending us?

I'm not sure I will fully understand the answer to that question until I get to heaven. It will be on my short list of questions. But I have no doubt that this is how God has set the whole thing up. It's this strategy that Jesus is referring to when he says, "The harvest is plentiful, but the workers are few" (Luke 10:2). When we really reflect on what Jesus is saying in that verse, we should feel equal parts inspired and uncomfortable.

Here's why it should make us uncomfortable. Jesus says that when we look at God, we see something equivalent to an abundant harvest that is ready to be poured out for all who want it. When we look at humanity, we see people who are desperately in need of it.

And yet . . . there is a gap. Despite having a God of abundance and a humanity in need, the plentiful harvest has not been fully realized. Why? Jesus says the reason is that there are too few workers.

There are certain parts of God's identity that I admittedly have trouble reconciling at times. It is not doubt, just lack of understanding. This is one of them. On one hand, I believe that God is sovereign, and I trust that if someone is hungry to know God, they will find God. On the other hand, Jesus draws a clear line between the availability of God's love and a shortage of missional workers who declare and demonstrate that love in a way that ensures those who need God actually find God.

That is what makes this verse uncomfortable for me. Jesus doesn't just talk about mission as something some of us may participate in if we are lucky. Jesus says that God's love is like an overflowing harvest, but not enough of us are taking that reality seriously. Mission really is God's one and only strategy—we either take the fact that we are sent as carriers of that love seriously, or we don't. Our decision has clear impact on the world's ability to know and respond to God. It shows how vital each one of us is to God's restoration project.

God's motivation is love, his attitude is abundance, and his strategy is to send us. We are the ones who make an invisible God visible to other people. We are the ones who translate the unseen reality of God's love into tangible expressions that other people can grab on to.

Isn't that incredible?

My guess is that you already have experienced this principle in your own life. I'll bet that part of your testimony points to God's love being made manifest in a way that you could concretely experience through another person.

When I ask someone to describe some of the ways that God's love has become tangible in their own life, they almost always say it came through another person.

> Sometimes it came through a parent who demonstrated God's love in a way that made them want to follow God.
>
> Sometimes it came through a conversation they had with a good friend or in a small group discussion.
>
> Sometimes it came through a worship experience or a song that touched them.
>
> Sometimes it came through a memorable sermon or a book that really spoke uniquely to them.

But it almost always came through a real person who demonstrated God's love in a way that took it out of the abstract and made it concrete.

What if these two foundations are true? What if mission is a love story that starts in the heart of God? What if God's strategy for making this love visible to the world is by sending you as a reflection of that love?

When you begin to see mission like this, it changes the way you view every day of your life; it can shift the way you interact with every moment. Any given moment could be the time God "sends" you to be a concrete reflection of his love in the life of someone who desperately needs to see God.

> You might be "sent" to volunteer for an afternoon with an organization whose cause you care about.
>
> You might be "sent" to share a kind word with someone who looks like they are having a rough day.
>
> You might be "sent" to write a note or send a text to someone God put on your mind.

> You might be "sent" to start a conversation about faith with someone you don't know.
> You might be "sent" to go on the search for new people at your church.

What remains constant is the reality that an invisible God becomes visible only when we step into the reality of mission. We see the unseen power of God's love through the concrete and practical actions of each other.

Foundation 3: Faith and Mission

At the core of both of these first two foundations is faith. Mission is the natural extension of "walking with God," the central metaphor of faith and intimacy (dimension 2 of faith in 3-D). When you are intimately connected to someone, you learn to love what they love and care about what they care about. This is as true in the human realm as it is in the divine. If we walk with God in intimacy, we will also walk with God in mission.

The apostle Paul used this kind of language to describe intimacy with God (as we saw in chapter 10). He used this kind of language to describe mission as well. In Ephesians 2:10 he said it like this: "For we are his workmanship, created in Christ Jesus for good works, which God prepared beforehand, that we should walk in them" (ESV).

When he says this, Paul is taking us back to the Garden and the image of walking intimately with God. By faith we are able to walk with God, and by faith we walk with God into the good works that have been created for us by Jesus Christ himself.

When Jesus talks about the Lord sending workers into his harvest field, he is making a similar faith connection for us. Even the word *workers* gets to the indispensable nature of faith and mission. Jesus uses it twice: "The harvest is plentiful, but the *workers* are few. Ask the Lord of the harvest, therefore, to send out *workers* into his harvest field" (Luke 10:2, emphasis added).

Some of us might hear that word and be tempted to silently grumble. *Here we go*, we think. *More work, more duty, more stuff I need to do that I am not currently doing.* But that is not at all what Jesus is referring to. In fact, this same word is used to describe the supernatural, life-giving power of God.

In John 5:17, Jesus says, "My Father is always at his work to this very day, and I too am *working*" (emphasis added).

When Jesus uses this same root word of *work* here, he is using it to describe the activity of God. In this specific instance, Jesus had just healed an invalid who had been ill for thirty-eight years. This would have been significant under any circumstance, but the fact that it had happened on his way to the Passover made it particularly noteworthy.

The healing happened at the Pool of Bethesda, a place where a number of men and women with physical ailments and disabilities would congregate. It was an unmistakable landmark, and Jesus and the disciples would have passed by it every year on their annual Passover trip. That was what made this particular healing puzzling for the onlookers.

If the invalid had been ill for thirty-eight years, then Jesus almost certainly had seen him before, probably multiple times. So why had Jesus not healed him on any of his previous trips? And for that matter, dozens of people were there struggling with various ailments. Why was this particular invalid the only one healed?

When pressed to explain, Jesus simply pointed to the relationship between faith and mission. "My Father is always at his work to this very day, and I too am working. . . . Very truly I tell you, the Son can do nothing by himself; he can do only what he sees his Father doing, because whatever the Father does the Son also does" (John 5:17, 19).

Nowhere in the Bible will you find a clearer connection between faith and mission than this. Jesus may have been the Son of God, but that didn't mean he could function outside of a spiritually intimate connection to the Father. Every healing, every supernatural sign, every Spirit-filled encounter—they all flowed from a faith connection to the heart of God. Jesus could only do what he saw the Father doing.

That becomes the pattern for every follower of Jesus as well.

Mission doesn't begin with us—mission begins in the heart of God. We begin with the assumption that God is always *working*. By faith we can learn to see what the Father is doing and how God is working.

Then we are "sent" to join God's work. We are sent as agents of God's love and grace; we are sent as ambassadors of God's reconciliation and justice.

This is the exciting news about mission. Mission is what connects the eternal, supernatural work of God with our everyday acts of love. Mission is what translates the mercy and grace of an unseen God into visible expressions that tangibly touch lives in meaningful ways.

Mission is what transforms regular people like us—in all of our inconsistency, insecurity, and unpredictability—into concrete and practical manifestations of the almighty God.

17

////////////////

Kingdom People

The purpose of Jesus's coming is to put the whole world right now, to renew and restore the creation, not to escape it. It is not just to bring personal forgiveness and peace, but also justice and shalom to the world.

Dr. Timothy Keller

Catching the mission bug is one of the most exciting things that ever happens to a Christ follower. When we realize that we have been created to make a difference in the lives of others, it helps rip us out of a shallow and stagnant experience of faith. When we begin to see that others' lives will be diminished if we do not live the life God has created us to live, we begin to receive each day as a new gift and new opportunity to be used by God.

That's why my eyes light up whenever someone from River City asks for some coaching or mentoring about how to step into greater degrees of faith and mission. Mission is what helped me break out of the persistent feeling that something was missing in my life, and I am filled with anticipation for the ways it might do the same for them.

Luke 10 has helped me understand how to live with a divine sense of mission, and it is the primary discipleship paradigm I use with others as they also attempt to take new steps in their journey of following Jesus into mission.

Most eager Christ followers want to jump right to the end when it comes to mission. They want to know exactly what they are supposed to do and are hungry for concrete and immediate next steps. That desire is understandable, and there is certainly a place for it. (I will spend the next two chapters exploring just that.)

Jesus gives very specific instructions to the first group of seventy-two disciples, and those instructions are equally applicable for us. But it's important to notice that he doesn't start there. He takes them through three stages as he guides them into a comprehensive understanding of mission, and both the stages and the order of them are important:

Stage 1: The foundations of mission—these are the three foundations covered in the previous chapter.

Stage 2: The theology of mission—that which informs how we think about mission.

Stage 3: The activity of mission—the specific instructions that guide our path as we take concrete steps into mission.

With that in mind, read the teaching that Jesus gives the initial seventy-two disciples on mission:

> After this the Lord appointed seventy-two others and sent them two by two ahead of him to every town and place where he was about to go. He told them, "The harvest is plentiful, but the workers are few. Ask the Lord of the harvest, therefore, to send out workers into his harvest field. Go! I am sending you out like lambs among wolves. Do not take a purse or bag or sandals; and do not greet anyone on the road.
>
> "When you enter a house, first say, 'Peace to this house.' If someone who promotes peace is there, your peace will rest on them; if not, it will return to you. Stay there, eating and drinking whatever they give you, for the worker deserves his wages. Do not move around from house to house.
>
> When you enter a town and are welcomed, eat what is offered to you. Heal the sick who are there and tell them, 'The kingdom of God has come near to you.'" (Luke 10:1–9)

After developing the three foundations of mission in the first two verses, Jesus moves into some in-depth theology. He refers to a pair of concepts that would have been familiar to the original seventy-two but are not always as familiar to us: shalom (peace) and the kingdom of God.

Shalom (Peace)

In verse 5, Jesus says the first thing the disciples should do when going out in mission is say, "Peace to this house," and then he uses the word "peace" again two more times.

What do you think of when you hear the word *peace*? Inner calm? The end of war? A person flashing a peace sign?

Peace was not an uncommon word in the vocabulary of Jesus. In the Beatitudes he says, "Blessed are the peacemakers, for they will be called children of God" (Matt. 5:9). And Jesus himself was prophesied as the coming "Prince of Peace" (Isa. 9:6) and as "our peace" (Mic. 5:4–5).

What is so significant about that word *peace*?

It is a derivative of the Hebrew word *shalom*. Shalom is still used by many Jews today as both a greeting and salutation, and it's an incredibly comprehensive and beautiful word. Yet despite its significance, it is not a concept that many Christ followers are familiar with.

My own underappreciation of shalom became vividly clear the first time I heard it. I was at a conference on evangelism that was being hosted at Wheaton College, and an African American pastor was giving the opening address. His words immediately caught my attention. "I am all about evangelism, and I boldly share my faith each and every time God gives me the opportunity. But as much as I care about evangelism, I'm also convinced that getting people 'saved' should never be our starting point when we interact with people who are searching for God. Our starting point should be shalom. That's one of the most important words in the entire Bible."

I remember hearing that and immediately thinking, "One of the most important words in the entire Bible? That's got to be an overstatement." I was twenty-five years old and had already been working at Willow Creek for a while. I had grown up in a variety of different church backgrounds, and I couldn't recall ever hearing the word shalom even one time. How could it possibly be one of the most important words in the Bible? And what did it have to do with evangelism?

He described shalom as a sweeping picture of comprehensive wholeness, a word that describes what the world would look like if it were under the reign of God. He said shalom represents the world at one—with God, with each other, and with creation. It represents harmony and flourishing across all domains—economic, social, racial, environmental, gender, and family peace.

He took us to one of the more famous passages about shalom in the Old Testament—Jeremiah 29. He said, "We know this passage for its famous ending—that God has a hope and great plan for our future. That's a great verse, but we forget that like just about everything else in the Bible, it is built on the idea of shalom."

If you are unfamiliar with Jeremiah 29, it's worth reading in its entirety. God tells the Jews, who have just been taken into exile to Babylon, to "seek the shalom" of the city that they had been carried into (see v. 7). God included some important markers of shalom to help guide their thought process:

- God told them to "build houses and settle down" (v. 5), which points to the economic dimension of shalom. To own your own home and to be able to provide for your family is one of the most basic elements of human dignity.

- God tells them to "plant gardens and eat what they produce" (v. 5), which points to the necessity of nutrition and access to healthy food, among other things.

- God tells them to "marry and have sons and daughters" (v. 6), which points to the centrality of healthy families as part of shalom seeking. Family was the first institution created by God, and when it falls apart, society tends to as well.

This pastor finished his talk by again underscoring the importance of shalom. He reminded us that shalom was the picture of God's design for the world and that it should inform all other aspects of mission.

He made the case that even evangelism cannot be fully understood outside of shalom. When we are talking to people about Jesus, it's important that they know that their spiritual identity is part of this bigger picture. They have been created with an intended design—a design that places God at the center of their being. When we reject God, we break shalom, and when we break shalom, God initiates a healing project to heal that which has been broken.

This was a profound concept for me, and shockingly new. How had I never heard about the centrality of shalom in the Bible?

I was grateful that this pastor planted a theological seed in my mind, because shalom eventually became a critical concept for me in gaining a holistic understanding of both faith and mission. I wondered how I had ever thought about important activities like evangelism and justice without first undergirding them with a vision of shalom. If we don't know what the world is supposed to look like under God's rule (shalom), then how can we know what it looks like for God to bring reconciliation and healing to that which has been broken?

And without shalom, how can we possibly understand what Jesus is saying when he tells the disciples to go and declare that "the kingdom of God has come near to you" (Luke 10:9)?

The Kingdom of God

The opening part of Jesus's missional instruction in Luke 10 is wrapped around the theme of shalom: "When you enter a house, first say, 'Peace to this house'" (v. 5). The disciples were to ground their sense of mission in shalom, and they were to bless people with this vision of comprehensive vitality and flourishing.

Jesus finished this missional instruction by instructing them to "heal the sick who are there and tell them, 'The kingdom of God has come near to you'" (v. 9).

This is another important theological concept. The language of "the kingdom of God" is quite familiar to some and less so to others. Regardless of how much exposure we've had to the phrase, it takes only basic observation of the New Testament to see that there was no concept that Jesus talked more about than the kingdom of God.

This remained true from the beginning until the end. Consider just a few examples spanning the lifetime of Jesus.

The beginning: Almost every Gospel account notes that Jesus launched his ministry with some type of proclamation of the kingdom of God. Mark's account is a good example: "The kingdom of God has come near. Repent and believe the good news!" (Mark 1:15).

The middle: His teachings and parables were dominated by the theme of the kingdom of God (see Matt. 13 for six straight parables illustrating the nature of the kingdom). Even the way Jesus prayed was connected to the kingdom of God. The most famous prayer in the Bible—the same one we recite together in a multitude of settings—has the nearness of the kingdom as its big theme: "Our Father in heaven, hallowed be your name, your kingdom come, your will be done, on earth as it is in heaven" (Matt. 6:9–10).

The end: Even in his resurrected state, Jesus kept the kingdom of God his primary focus. During the forty days between his resurrection and his final ascension to heaven, this remained his subject matter: "After his suffering, he presented himself to them and gave many convincing proofs that he was alive. He appeared to them over a period of forty days and spoke about the kingdom of God" (Acts 1:3).

The "kingdom of God" is really just a natural extension of shalom. The phrase comes from the Greek word *basileia*, which translates as "rule" or "authority."

When Jesus is King, we experience shalom. Whatever the King touches becomes redeemed and moves toward fullness of life. The markers of shalom become abundance, beauty, respect, dignity, equality, health, vitality, and holistic flourishing.

But when Jesus is not our king, we experience a loss of shalom. This can manifest as anything from internal struggle (depression, anxiety, insecurity, self-centeredness) to physical struggle (sickness, disease), neighborhood struggle (violence, crime, poor educational options, lack of access to healthy food), national struggle (racism, oppression, lack of access to jobs or capital), and global struggle (war, famine, abject poverty).

Our intuition tells us that God created the world to work a certain way, and our spirits hope and pray that Jesus is working to restore creation to its original potential. We "groan inwardly," along with the rest of creation, as we await this restoration (see Rom. 8:22–23).

The Garden of Eden was our first glimpse of shalom. We got to see what the world looked like when God was in control. We got to see how God related to humans and how the entire created ecosystem reflected God's glory. We all possess a distant memory of that shalom, and everything inside of us longs to return to that.

Though sin and selfishness wreaked havoc on that shalom, that was not the end of the story. God initiated a healing and restoration project, and the death and resurrection of Jesus Christ was the pinnacle of that plan. Jesus is "the image of the invisible God," as Paul says in Colossians 1:15, and through him the invisible God becomes visible for all of us to see.

Through the resurrected Jesus the kingdom of God is now being ushered in, and that is a full-scale restoration project. There is no aspect of our world that is untouched by Jesus, as Paul says in the next verse: "For in him all things were created: things in heaven and on earth, visible and invisible, whether thrones or powers or rulers or authorities; all things have been created through him and for him" (Col. 1:16).

The manifestation of the kingdom of God is initiated by Jesus, and his goal is fullness of life: "For God was pleased to have all his fullness dwell in him, and through him to reconcile to himself all things, whether things on earth or things in heaven, by making peace through his blood, shed on the cross" (Col. 1:19–20).

When Jesus shed his blood on the cross, he began the process of "making peace," the same word that he used when sending the disciples out on mission. This is what begins to bring the whole picture together. When we pray about, talk about, and work toward the kingdom of God, we are joining with this process of Jesus making peace through his blood, shed on the cross.

///////////

I know that right about this point, all these words can start to feel overwhelming. Peace, shalom, kingdom of God . . . how are we supposed to remember all this when it comes to mission?

If these were questions that we had to get right on the big test to get to heaven, I would feel really nervous. But they are not. These weighty theological truths belong to Jesus, and he doesn't expect us to understand them—at least not without his help.

I love how Dallas Willard talks about this in his book *Knowing Christ Today*. In the book he recounts a conversation where he was asked how a normal, everyday Christian is supposed to grasp a complicated concept like the kingdom of God. How is it that we enter into life in the kingdom? Here is how Willard answered:

> We must humble ourselves and become like little children (Matt. 18:3–5). That means we must be turned around ("converted") from the normal human attitude, the attitude that says we are in charge of our life and that we are quite competent and capable of managing it on our own. Little children, on the other hand, come to others for guidance and help and simply presume upon them for it. They have no other option, and they do not think they do.[1]

I love that quote, because it flips our natural instinct on its head. We live with a weird mix of fear and pride when it comes to mission, and we assume that we need to become "quite competent" and "capable of managing it on our own." But that is not what Jesus asks of us. Instead, he asks that we would humble ourselves and become like little children. Only then can we really grasp the deep meaning of these rich theological ideas like shalom and the kingdom of God.

This is the same thing that Jesus said to Nicodemus, who came to Jesus under the cover of night in search of answers that had previously eluded him. Nicodemus said, "Rabbi, we know that you are a teacher who has come from God. For no one could perform the signs you are doing if God were not with him" (John 3:2).

It was obvious to Nicodemus that Jesus had "come from God" and that there was some type of ongoing, supernatural connection between them. Nicodemus could see that nobody would be able to do what Jesus was doing "if God were not with him."

What Jesus told Nicodemus next completely shocked him: "No one can see the kingdom of God unless they are born again" (John 3:3).

Nicodemus was completely disoriented by this. As a leading Pharisee and member of the Jewish ruling council, Nicodemus was a paragon of religious virtue. He was dutiful, respectful, moral, and pious. When he approached Jesus, I'll bet he was expecting to hear something like this: "Nicodemus, you are a great guy and a devoted religious man. You are almost there."

Instead, Jesus essentially said, "It's all about the kingdom of God, Nicodemus. Without me, and without the renewing power of the Holy Spirit, you can't even see the kingdom."

For a person whose understanding of Christianity is built on impressing God with their list of good deeds, this would be really bad news. But if what we hunger for is an authentic experience of the divine, then this is incredibly good news.

The reign of Jesus, the restoration of shalom, the materialization of the kingdom of God—these are concepts that we are not able to fully grasp in the natural realm. Our five natural senses cannot fully absorb their meaning.

We need Jesus to lead us by faith into the realm of the spiritual, the realm of the kingdom of God. Faith is what allows us to "see" that which is already surrounding us. Like the disciples on the road to Emmaus who recognized Jesus when he broke the bread, or like Mary Magdalene who recognized Jesus after he called her name in the garden, we have our eyes opened by faith to the reality of both the King and the kingdom.

This is what this second stage of Jesus's teaching on mission is pointing toward. To be sent by God into mission has everything to do with shalom and the kingdom of God. Mission has at its starting point the vision of shalom—a vision of God's intended design. Mission is the conviction that Jesus is bringing the kingdom of God from heaven to earth and that we become the concrete expression of that coming kingdom.

It is only against these theological backdrops that the two activities of mission really make sense.

18

//////////////

Witness

The most basic meaning of evangelism is to be a person who connects the invisible reality of God to the visible world of someone that is not a Christian. Therefore, it is not foundationally about a skill, but rather a way of life that overflows into your everyday life.

Erwin McManus

I could barely believe it was happening. While in the middle of a busy rush at Starbucks, one of my fellow baristas discovered that my "real job" was working at Willow Creek. Acting as if she had never come in contact with a live pastor before, she began squealing with delight, telling every customer and employee of her discovery. This revelation caused a spontaneous spiritual combustion at the store, and I listened as a group of people circled around the espresso bar and regaled me with stories of their spiritual history.

Selma went first. "I think Christianity has an important place in society. I don't personally follow it, but I figure, whatever makes you happy, do it."

Matt quickly followed, the painful interactions he had experienced in his spiritual journey clearly showing. "Christianity is for simple-minded people. When they talk to you, they act as if you are a robot.

They have an agenda they are trying to promote, and if you don't agree with them, they are done with you."

Tatia thought about Matt's comments for a moment and then added her own. "I don't know if that's what bothers me so much. What really gets under my skin is that all the church wants from you is your money."

Justin put the finishing touches on the conversation, seeming to summarize everyone's feelings when he said, "Look, we all know that 'God' is out there at some level, but no one has a right to tell another person what 'God' looks like for them. Each person is free to express that however they want, but they should keep their opinions to themselves."

Such was my baptism by fire into the mission of being a witness. As I sat there listening to Selma, Matt, Tatia, and Justin energetically share their perspectives about spirituality, I just had to sit back and smile. How in the world did I end up in this situation? *Only God*, I thought.

I began to reflect on how quickly the last three years had unfolded and what a big role mission had played in bringing me to this point.

It had all started when I met Thad. I still marveled at the imprint he had left on my life simply by listening for the voice of God asking, "Whom shall I send? And who will go for us?" (Isa. 6:8). Because he obeyed God, my life had been forever changed.

It was the simplicity of that act that most inspired me to seriously consider mission. If Thad saying hello to a stranger could change a life like that, then why couldn't I do the same? I was ready to give mission a try, and like Thad, I decided to practice at the Axis service. He had talked about the importance of shifting from a "me-first" mentality to a "mission-first" mentality, and he swore that it would change a person's life. So that is exactly what I attempted to do.

Coming in with this lens gave me a whole new perspective. It was amazing to see that even a church service like Axis matched both sides of Jesus's description of mission in Luke 10:2: "The harvest is plentiful, but the workers are few."

One of the strongest features of Axis was its ability to draw spiritual seekers who were disconnected from God and alienated from church. It was amazing how many of them would visit each week. Clearly there was abundant opportunity to reach people who were searching and to help them take next steps in their new journey.

And yet, in the words of Jesus, "the workers" were few. Despite having a room filled with spiritual seekers, too few Christ followers were ready to step out of their comfort zone, start a conversation, and live with this sense of missional purpose and meaning.

This shortage of workers was certainly not a result of lack of effort from Thad. He was a constant motivator and tried to inspire every one of us at Axis to seize the opportunity that had been set before us. He would consistently remind us how rare it was to have a church service filled with so many spiritual seekers. God had entrusted it to us, and Thad pleaded with us to take the stewardship of that opportunity seriously.

But much to his disappointment, very few people seemed to be up for it. There were just too many hurdles to overcome—fear, pride, apathy, indifference, insecurity, and on and on the list seemed to go.

I was sick of living "me-first," though, so I told Thad I was ready for the challenge. I asked him to show me the way, and I would join him each Saturday night to roam the perimeter of the room, asking God to send us to someone who might be disconnected, lost, hurting, or alienated.

That is where the journey of mission began for me, and I have fond memories of that era. I remember how much initial fear and anxiety I felt, for reasons that I have already shared. But I also remember being filled with meaning and purpose for the first time, and that more than made up for the discomfort I so often felt when leaving my comfort zone.

As the months passed, God began to build on that experience. Becoming bold within the Axis service was my 101 level training for mission, and now I could sense God moving in my heart for a new assignment. I started sensing a consistent stirring from God around the words from Isaiah 6:8: "Whom shall I send? And who will go for us?" I thought I was already being responsive to this call by being so intentional at Axis, but it seemed that God was describing something beyond that now. I felt like Abraham, whose story in Hebrews 11 says that he was sent by faith, "even though he did not know where he was going" (v. 8).

This would not be the last time I felt that combination of God strongly stirring in me while also having no idea toward what or where. It was a bit frustrating at the beginning, but I eventually realized that this is a key attribute of the faith and intimacy dimension.

Mission is a by-product of an intimate walk with God. As we grow closer to God, he shares the "secrets" of his heart with us (see Jer. 33:3 and Ps. 25:14). One of those intimate secrets is where he is at work (see John 5:17) and how it is that we can follow Jesus into mission there. These feel to me almost like special calls or assignments, and they become one of the ways that I most intimately experience God in my life.

At that time, my small group leader had encouraged me to view the vague stirring that I was feeling as something to be cherished and nurtured, not frustrated by. He urged me to be open to the possibility that maybe the point of the stirring was to move me closer to God and that it could double as an opportunity for some quality time alone praying and reflecting.

This struck me as insightful, so I chose to act on it. I will never forget the night I was sitting in the neighborhood Starbucks, thinking about this. It was the closest Starbucks to Willow Creek, and I was a regular patron there. It was where I both did my homework (I was in seminary now) and had many of my quiet times. I wrote this in my journal:

> God, I feel like you are moving in me, stirring me toward some type of new assignment. I've tried to be faithful to come to Axis each Saturday night looking for new people, and I have grown so much by taking risks with them. But now I feel like you are moving me to something new. What is it? I sense that you want me to be a witness, but to who? And to where?

I took a break from writing and sat back in my chair. As I looked around the coffee shop, I felt God confirm what I was suddenly sensing. It was out of the box and way different from what I was expecting, but I sensed God telling me to apply for a job at Starbucks. The friendships I was forming with the staff there could be only peripheral if I remained a customer, but what if I actually worked there?

At first I resisted, because it made no practical sense. I had already taken this new job at Willow Creek; I had ongoing responsibilities with my technology company; and I had begun taking seminary classes at night. My schedule didn't seem to have much margin.

Yet God continued to stir my heart, so I figured I would see if the manager was in and inquire about any openings. If she said no, that would solve my dilemma.

She was indeed there and, to my surprise, was able to meet with me immediately. I told her of my potential interest, though I immediately emphasized that I already had a very busy schedule and that I doubted it would work out. It wasn't exactly the most stellar interview I've ever had.

She said, "This might work. Do you think you could do a couple of mornings a week?"

Suddenly this conversation was going in the wrong direction. I have always been a night owl and have a corresponding allergy to early mornings. I think I told her something very similar to that.

Somehow she moved past all my hesitation and said, "This could be perfect! We only have one part-time opening, and it's the opening shift, two or three mornings a week."

I begrudgingly asked, "And how early is the opening shift?"

"Five a.m.," she gleefully squealed. "But don't worry, I'll be here with you"—as if that was my biggest problem.

Ugh, I thought. *Morning people!*

The job was mine if I wanted it, but there was still one last hurdle. I had to get permission from Nancy, my boss at Willow Creek, before I could accept the position at Starbucks. I was really not feeling that early start time and hoped that Nancy would give me an out.

But Nancy was no help. She said, "That sounds great! I think God is really leading you in this direction, and I think you should do it. Besides, you might not only impact the people who work there—think of the ways you might impact our staff. Most of the spiritual seekers we talk to are already inside the walls of the church. You will now be in everyday community with spiritual seekers outside the walls of the church."

Though Nancy failed to provide the excuse I was looking for, she did give me something priceless in its place. The differentiation she made between spiritual seekers "inside" the walls of the church and "outside" the walls of the church caused a lightbulb to come on for me.

I didn't have words for it at the time, but I was already starting to fall into the same trap that besets many of the men and women who work at churches. In fact, I'll share a little secret about us pastor/minister/ clergy types with you, one we are quite embarrassed by: though we go to seminary to get trained all about this stuff, most of us are not meaningfully connected to the mission of God outside the walls of the church. We get so caught up with the demands placed upon us within the church that we end up missing out on the opportunity to join the mission of God outside the walls.

It leads to one of the great ironies of evangelism: the ones who are most trained to have spiritual conversations have the least amount of contact with nonbelievers, and the ones who have the most contact tend to be filled with fear and insecurity and doubt, and often struggle with their own credibility to have these conversations.

It's important to acknowledge this dynamic, because the mission of God is primarily taking place outside of the walls of churches, not inside. Obviously it's important that churches are run well and can nurture people spiritually and build a sense of community, and at some level that's all part of God's mission. But when we look at the witness element of mission—the call to go and talk to people about the kingdom of God—this is something happening outside of the walls.

That's where Jesus spent most of his time. He was always moving to the fringes, to the most irreligious places in society. While he also cared about those who were more traditionally religious, his undying passion remained for the tax collectors, the prostitutes, and the members of society who had been rejected by the religious institution. In Luke 19:10 he succinctly summarized this passion by saying, "The Son of Man came to seek and to save the lost."

The bulk of your time is likely not spent at church—it's spent in the workplace, at school, in social environments, or in interactions with extended family. Those happen to be the places that most need a witness to the kingdom of God. They are also the places that are furthest away from the reach of most pastors and clergy. They will never be reached without everyday Christ followers who take mission seriously.

That is why I believe faith and mission is such an important dimension to embrace, both for your own growth and for the growth of others. It's important for the faith journey of others because they are already asking all kinds of "kingdom" questions. They don't use that label, but the issues that people at your work, school, and social hangouts are wrestling with are deeply spiritual, aren't they? They are trying to sort out what direction they are going to go in life, who they should date and marry, whether or not they should make that job switch, and where they are going to turn for guidance on morals and values. They need someone to talk through these important questions with, and very few of them are going to consider going to a church to find that wisdom.

Talking about the kingdom isn't just important for their faith—it's important for yours too. That's what I found out, maybe more than anything, during my time at Starbucks.

If the success of my three-year stint was measured by the number of conversions that occurred, then I was a failure. Not one of those Starbucks employees became a Christian during my tenure, despite numerous spiritual conversations and even a handful of visits to Axis. I was very aware of this, since I was in a culture where things tended to be measured by end results. I often wondered if anything meaningful was actually happening with all those hours I was working at Starbucks, and it was easy for me to feel discouraged by what I perceived as a lack of fruit. Luckily, one of the mentors who knew me well and watched my journey closely helped me see how this was impacting not only the Starbucks baristas but also my own growth. He said,

Don't ever forget, mission is about faith and spiritual vitality. If mission were just about counting conversions, it would be nothing more than a legalistic, soulless task. That is not what God is about. Mission is about being tuned in to this love story that is happening all around us and being sensitive to the voice of God as he sends us into that story as an agent of that love. I've watched how your friends at Starbucks have changed. Three years ago they had a very low view of Christians and church. But they've come with you to Axis, they've seen how faith has shaped you, and they've had lots of great spiritual conversations. The love of God is more real to them now than it was then, and that has to be considered a huge success. But even more, I've seen how much you have changed as you've worked at Starbucks. Building these new friendships and having these intense conversations has brought so much new vitality to your spiritual life. I think you needed them as much as they needed you.

Those words meant a lot and helped me to see just how much this era at Starbucks had meant to my own faith. It helped me remember how reciprocal the mission of being a witness is. When it is working right, it stretches the faith of everyone involved. The faith of the Christ follower is stretched and deepened as they step out of their comfort zone and tell people about life in God's kingdom. The faith of his or her conversation partner is stretched as they wrestle with what it means to be right with God and right with the world.

Though my time at Starbucks wrapped up after three years, my commitment to living with a heightened sense of faith and mission did not. By this point I had come to the conclusion that listening for God to ask, "Whom shall I send?" was one of the most transformational things a Christ follower can do to revolutionize his or her spiritual life.

What started in the Axis service had now become my prayer at Starbucks as well. And what had been my prayer at Starbucks was becoming my prayer everywhere. I was single at the time, and most nights I was doing something social. Building off of the experience I had at Starbucks, I began to pray every time I went to a party or an event that God would send me into a conversation with someone who was ready to talk about the kingdom if the timing was right.

I eventually got married and tried to carry that same mission-first mentality into our new lifestyle. We had dogs and would often take them to the dog park. It might sound silly, but every time we headed over there, I would pray the missional prayer—I would ask God to send me into conversation with one of the other dog owners if the timing was right.

When we go to events with other couples, or when we take our little kids to play groups, I start by getting myself in a mission-first mindset. It changes the way I enter into any environment. I don't obsess about it, but I also want to maintain a high degree of spiritual sensitivity. If God is always working, then whatever group I'm in at the moment could be one of the places God is doing his best work. I don't want to miss the opportunity to participate if it's there.

I hope and pray that this will come to describe your way of life too. In an earlier era for me, it was about talking to people after the Axis service, and in another era, it was taking a job at Starbucks, and then it eventually turned into an everyday awareness of mission that has ranged from dog parks to toddler playdates.

They all stem from the same thing—from a belief that Jesus sends us out as witnesses to talk about the kingdom of God. We are sent out to make God's love real for people who are searching for that love.

One of the things I have noticed about my journey in becoming a witness is the gentle way that Jesus has pushed me out of my comfort zone. I have always felt fear, but not so much that I couldn't move forward if I so chose. If my initial assignment had been to lead a Bible study at my work or to intentionally apply for a job at Starbucks, that would have been overwhelming for me. So God allowed me to start small and to gain courage with each successive assignment.

This is one of the cool things about following Jesus as the author and pioneer of faith. He customizes this journey for each one of us. He knows that his Father is at work, and he knows that each of us has a unique contribution to make to that work. Jesus goes just far enough down the path to make us uncomfortable, but not so far down the path that we can't realistically follow him there.

I'm discovering this principle once again right now. I'm proof that fear never goes away and that fresh waves of great faith are consistently necessary. Jesus is authoring and pioneering in my life right now, stirring me toward new expressions of being a witness once again.

I was recently invited to join a group of "social innovators" in Chicago. I didn't even know what that label meant when I received the invitation. The organizer told me that it was something I shouldn't miss—he said it's a group filled with some of the brightest and most active people in our city.

When I read the list of some of the other people who were invited, I immediately felt intimidated. It was a who's who of people involved in innovative programs for addressing ongoing urban problems. I recognized many of the names, as they are well known for their amazing efforts around homelessness, joblessness, education reform, and health and nutrition.

When I arrived at the first meeting, I was nervous. There were close to thirty people there, and I didn't know any of them. Fear was strong, and the most courageous thing I could do was just stand there and not walk right back out. Fortunately, that feeling didn't last long, and some of the more connected people there reached out to me. Through them I began to meet the other guests, and things started rolling.

Most of the conversations were small talk, but something became apparent even within the semisuperficial conversations. Despite the fact that the common bond in the room was a commitment to social good, I was pretty certain I was the only Christian there. This was disappointing, but it matched a growing trend that I've noticed. For whatever reason, a lot of churches talk about the kingdom of God but don't include justice and compassion as part of that conversation. And then there are a lot of people who talk about justice and compassion but don't include the church in that conversation. This meeting was just one more place that revealed this fragmentation.

The organizer eventually asked everyone to sit down, and he began to give a vision for his agenda. He had found a philanthropist to pay for these monthly dinners with the purpose of getting top social innovators from around the city to network, encourage, and stimulate each other's thinking. This group represented what he believed was the crème de la crème, and he told us that it was his hope that some great friendships would form over time.

To kick things off, he asked if every person in the room would stand up and introduce themselves. He asked us to keep it to thirty seconds, answering this question: "What are you doing around social innovation, and why should everybody else in the room know about that?"

Until this point I had been suppressing a small level of fear, but now it was in full bloom. I felt insecure and out of place in this room. And now I was going to have to introduce myself using a term I had never heard or used to describe myself! I was the only pastor, and almost the only Christian, in a roomful of people who didn't think particularly highly of church. How was I supposed to convince anyone I was a social innovator?

I don't think Jesus ever stops taking us to that intersection of faith and fear, and I was there once again. I felt my heart rate increasing, so

I began to pray that God would calm my spirit and center my mind. As my heart rate began to slow down, I sensed God simply bringing Isaiah 6:8 to mind: "Whom shall I send? And who will go for us?" I smiled, because this seems to be where God always brings me back to.

If I could put words to what I heard God whispering to me, it would have sounded like this: "Don't forget about who I am or what I am about. I am trying to redeem and reconcile all things to myself, including this group of men and women, whom I love. I am at work in this place, and I want my love to become real and tangible here. You have not been sent here to try to impress people or to prove yourself as an innovator. You have been sent here to represent my love and to tell people about the kingdom of God."

I share that because so often my own ego and my own self gets mixed up with the message, and one of the ways God graciously moves me forward is by helping me sort those out from each other. I would have been very tempted to try to present myself in a way that made me look more attractive to this group than I really was, and I felt God freeing me from that burden. It's so much work to present a cleaned-up version of yourself and so much less work just to be you and to let God do the work.

I was still feeling nervous about how to introduce myself using the social innovator label, and I felt God whisper one more thing: "Don't forget, the greatest social innovator who ever lived was Jesus Christ. When he declared the kingdom of God was coming near, he launched a social movement that would never be matched."

I finally felt in sync with God and understood why I was there. These were all men and women who were trying to understand the kingdom, even if they weren't asking that question or using that word. I just needed to be ready and available for any opportunities that God might open up.

When it was finally my turn to speak, I stood up and said, "My name is Daniel Hill. Oftentimes there seems to be a disconnect between faith and social innovation, and that is the field I come from. I try to help people find that the greatest levels of social innovation happen only when they are rooted in faith."

Once the presentations were over, a woman from the other end of the room headed straight for me. She asked me to elaborate further on what I meant by the connection between faith and social innovation. I talked very straightforwardly with her about my role as a pastor and the mission of River City. I shared my belief that faith should be what informs our social work and my disappointment that the connection between those two is often hard for people to see. We talked about the confusion of churches that don't emphasize social justice and social justice people who don't think about church.

It was an incredible conversation. She had grown up in church but hadn't been back since high school. She was now the head of a consulting firm that specialized in social innovation and had always struggled to reconcile what she did with the possibility of God. On top of that, she was a new mom and was starting to think about how she would talk about faith with her two young children.

We had hardly finished our conversation when another gentleman took her place across the table from me. He had been listening in and was particularly fascinated with the fact that River City is located in a poor neighborhood that has a large African American population. He had grown up in Detroit, in a neighborhood just like ours, and he talked about the joys of his upbringing but also some of the unbelievably challenging obstacles he had faced.

He was considered one of the success stories from his neighborhood. Most of his other friends had gotten caught up in the many trappings that come from the net of poverty, and he lamented that. But with the steady oversight of a loving grandmother, he had gotten good grades and won a prestigious scholarship to a top college. That later turned into a graduate program at Northwestern, which he was just finishing. He felt really happy about his accomplishments but also felt a deep loss of identity as well. He was completely disconnected from his neighborhood in Detroit and wondered out loud if, in chasing the American dream, he had left behind both his faith and his culture.

He talked for thirty straight minutes, almost as if I wasn't there. When he finished, he apologized, as if he had taken precious time from me. I told him I was blessed to have heard his story and his struggle, and I encouraged him to honor the tension he was feeling. When I told him that it might be God calling this man back to himself, he started to squirm. "I'm not quite ready to call it God," he said. With a mischievous smile he added, "First I need to pay off all my student debt, and then I can start thinking about God." We went on to talk about other topics and then exchanged business cards, promising to stay in touch.

When the event finally finished, I grabbed a drink with the guy who had organized the whole thing. We talked about the event itself for a while, and then I told him about the two conversations I'd had. I was surprised at the level of interest the two people had showed in faith and asked my friend why he thought that was.

He was a Christ follower, and his faith was part of what had compelled him to organize this event. Still, I was surprised by his answer: "It's the shalom thing."

I rarely hear other people use that word, so I was thrilled to hear something right out of my own vocabulary. I asked him to expand on what he meant. He said,

> Every person in that room knows that the world was created to work in a certain way, but that it's broken. That's why they do what they do. They are sincere, well-meaning people who are trying to do their part to make things right. But even though they are "experts" in their respective fields, they all know that something is still missing. They know that the particular problem they are trying to solve is ultimately just a symptom of larger problems. And they know that the larger problems are really difficult to address and probably can't be solved without some type of spiritual solution. There is an inner emptiness that they sense, and they are looking for ways to address it. That's why I wanted you here. I knew that you would have credibility with them because of your work at River City, and I knew that you would be sensitive as to how you approached that topic with them. I knew it would be a match.

When I walked away from that meeting, I felt a deep connection to the presence of God. It was one of those God-ordained moments—one of those moments where the work of the Father became clear to me, and I had the privilege of participating in that work.

As I drove home, I reflected upon the last fifteen-plus years of doing my best to live with a sense of faith and mission. I remembered how scary it was for me to talk to people at the Axis service as a twenty-two-year-old, and I smiled at what seemed like such a huge mountain of fear back then. I remembered both the fear and the excitement that

I felt the first time I reached out as a witness within Axis and was amazed at how similar I felt at this meeting with social innovators in Chicago.

I thanked God for the honor of being able to participate in mission and surrendered myself to the ministry of Jesus once again. I told God that I wanted to continue to learn about the kingdom, to bear witness to the kingdom, and to live into the promise of the Lord's Prayer—to see God's kingdom come on earth as it is in heaven.

That is my same prayer for you. I pray that you will allow the author and pioneer of faith to take you into deeper and deeper knowledge of himself and of the kingdom that he has come to bring to fruition. I pray that you will experience it in your own life and that you will grow in courage and in your ability to bear witness to that which Jesus reveals to you.

We don't always understand how stepping out as a witness will impact the world around us. But my friend who invited me to this event serves as a living example of how God is orchestrating things behind the scenes. God is moving us, guiding us, and using us. It isn't our job to be able to discern the exact point at which our witness hits home. It's our job to simply be a witness and trust that he knows exactly where he is aiming our outer expression of faith into the lives of others.

19

///////////////

Neighbors

When you witness for justice you are expressing the deepest yearn-
ings and values of people, even if they are not conscious of those
values.

Dr. Robert Franklin

Who is my neighbor?

That is the question that launched one of the most famous parables
in the entire Bible. We commonly refer to it as "The Good Samaritan,"
and it is found in Luke 10:25–37.

The man asking this question was an expert in Old Testament law,
and his intentions were as much about justifying himself as about
genuinely seeking truth (see v. 29). The conversation had begun with
an obtuse question about eternal life, and rather than getting pulled
into this man's snare, Jesus flipped the question back to him: "What
is written in the Law?" (v. 26).

This was a brilliant response on many levels. The expert in the law
knew the answer was obvious and unavoidable. Even the kids would get
this one right. The most important prayer in Judaism was the Shema,
and at the center was what we now call the Great Commandment.
So the expert in the law answered, "'Love the Lord your God with

all your heart and with all your soul and with all your strength and with all your mind'; and, 'Love your neighbor as yourself'" (v. 27).

Jesus affirmed his answer, then said, "Do this and you will live" (v. 28).

This was not how the law expert expected this conversation to unfold, and he grasped for a follow-up question. Looking to "justify himself," he asked Jesus a final question: "And who is my neighbor?" (v. 29).

The reverberations of that question are still being felt two thousand years later. In fact, few questions in the Bible carry more weight, and when Luke places it within the context of chapter 10, he shows its importance in at least two different ways.

First, we are reminded that the question "Who is my neighbor?" is central to the essence of Christianity. In Luke 10 we see that it was the center of the Hebrew understanding of Scripture, and in Matthew 22:34–40 Jesus acknowledges the Shema as the greatest commandment of all. It is not possible to think of Christian discipleship without also thinking of the command to love our neighbor.

Second, we now see that the question "Who is my neighbor?" is also central to a life of mission. Just verses earlier Jesus sent out the disciples to heal the sick as a sign of the kingdom. Now, immediately following their return, Jesus tells the story of the Good Samaritan. This is Luke's way of fleshing out what the second activity of mission looks like. Seeking shalom, pursuing justice, acting as agents of healing—these can all be integrated under the heading of loving our neighbor.

It's likely that you are already familiar with the story of the Good Samaritan, so I am not going to retell it in great detail. What I would like to do instead is look at it through the lens of faith and mission. At the end of the story Jesus asks the law expert, "Which of these three do you think was a neighbor to the man who fell into the hands of robbers?" (v. 36).

The answer is the Samaritan—he becomes the archetype for mission. Jesus could have described a neighbor in any way he chose, and these are the details he decided to emphasize. We see some fundamental traits that describe the archetypal neighbor, and these are the same traits that will guide our path as we follow Jesus into the second activity of a missional Christian.

Three character traits are of particular importance in this parable: compassion, reconciliation, and justice.

Trait 1: Compassion—Seeing the World as God Does

This is the most straightforward of all the qualities that Jesus highlights: "But a Samaritan, as he journeyed, came to where he was, and when he saw him, he had compassion" (v. 33 ESV).

For me, *compassion* was always one of those squishy words that were void of much meaning. I thought of it as a generic, vanilla description of people who were kindhearted and gentle in demeanor.

But that doesn't land anywhere near the full meaning of the word that Jesus used to describe the primary trait exhibited by the Samaritan. There are a handful of different Greek words that can all translate into English as *compassion*, and Jesus chose the strongest to make his point: *splagchnizomai*. This sounds more like a complicated Italian dish than a word to describe compassion, but despite its difficult sound, it's a beautiful word.

Some versions translate *splagchnizomai* into English as *indignant*, which comes from the same root word as *dignity*, and that puts its own unique twist on what Jesus was saying. *Splagchnizomai* describes a fusion of emotions. There is compassion and concern for the person who has been injured or oppressed, but it is also combined with a righteous anger toward the root cause of the problem. In a story like this, *splagchnizomai* becomes a vivid way to describe the reaction of the Samaritan. He felt both compassion for the man who had been beaten and anger toward that which hurt him and stripped him of his dignity (i.e., the robbers who beat him and the unsafe corridor he had to travel through).

That alone makes it a cool word, but the way Jesus uses it here takes it to a whole other level. *Splagchnizomai* is used a number of times throughout the Bible, and it's used almost exclusively to describe the compassion that Jesus feels toward us. And yet, in the telling of this parable, Jesus borrows a word that is typically reserved only for him and uses it instead to describe the Samaritan. In the most explicit teaching in the Bible on the topic, Jesus says that a missional neighbor is one who feels the exact same compassion or *splagchnizomai* as he himself feels.

By saying this, Jesus draws a straight line between faith and intimacy (dimension 2) and faith and mission (dimension 3). Before the Samaritan could react with an outward, missional response, he first needed to have an internal, intimate connection to God.

And to ensure the point is clearly made, Jesus doubles up with the phrase that immediately precedes the compassion: "But a Samaritan, as he journeyed, came to where he was, and when he *saw him*, he had compassion" (Luke 10:33 ESV, emphasis added).

The reason that the Samaritan was able to feel the same type of compassion toward this victim that Jesus feels toward us is because he could first *see* him. In that moment there was a direct sync between the vision of God and the vision of the Samaritan. He saw what the Father saw, and he responded accordingly.

This follows in line with some of the other faith passages we've explored in this section on mission. It's what Jesus was talking about in John 5:19 when he said, "The Son can do nothing by himself; he can do only what he sees his Father doing." It's what Jesus was trying to get Nicodemus to understand when he said, "No one can see the kingdom of God unless they are born again" (John 3:3).

Faith gives us the ability to see the world as God sees it. Faith allows us to see the kingdom of God and to grow in understanding of that. Faith allows us to see what the Father is doing and to participate in that. Faith allows us to see someone who has been unjustly treated and to feel the exact same compassion toward him or her that God feels.

That's a pretty breathtaking reality, and it should alter the way we view mission. We are invited to see the world as God sees it and then respond accordingly.

Trait 2: Reconciliation—Moving toward the Other

Many of us are so used to this story being called "The Good Samaritan" that we miss just how unsettling this idea would have been for those who first heard it. For the first-century Jews who were huddled around Jesus, compassion would not have been the main thing that they heard. Instead, they would have been so shocked and dismayed by the fact that Jesus established the racial/cultural identity of the hero as Samaritan that they would have almost certainly missed everything else.

It was an interesting strategy by Jesus. Nobody would have protested a story about compassion. That was obviously a big point that Jesus was trying to make, so why not just stop there? Why not zero in on compassion and ignore the cultural background of the neighbor?

Or why not give him a more culturally neutral background, one that wouldn't elicit feelings of anger or resentment? Or even better yet, why not just make the hero a Jew? That would solve everything. One Jew gets beaten and left for dead, and another Jew comes and saves him. That would have gotten a good "amen," and everyone could have gone out and tried to be more compassionate.

But as important as the point about the need for compassion was, it was not enough for Jesus. He wanted them to wrestle with reconciliation as well. So he chose a "Samaritan," someone whom Jewish teachers weren't even allowed to utter the name of out loud. That's raising the stakes!

This is not the first time that Jesus leaned into the Samaritan/Jewish divide to highlight the importance of reconciliation. In John 4, Jesus intentionally led the disciples through Samaria, and his own disciples were amazed that he would talk to anyone of Samaritan descent (see v. 27). When Jesus was dialoguing with the Samaritan woman, she was equally shocked and referred to the historical feud that divided them: "Jews do not associate with Samaritans" (John 4:9). We also see Samaria named as part of the Great Commission (see Acts 1:8), and when Samaritans respond to Philip in Acts 8, it becomes a key sign of the coming kingdom of God.

Because this story has had such a significant influence on my understanding of mission, I've done a lot of research on the bitter divide between the Jews and the Samaritans. Knowing some of their history has added a lot to this parable.

The bad blood began in 722 BC, when the Jews were captured and taken into captivity by the Assyrians. Most of the Jews separated themselves from the Assyrians to protect their cultural identity, but a small number of Jews intermarried with the local Assyrians. A new generation of blended-heritage children was born, and they would be forever defined as Samaritans—half Jew, half Assyrian.

The animosity between these groups was evident almost immediately. Most Jews at that time viewed the intermarrying with the Assyrians as an affront to God, and the fact that Samaritans mixed together the religious practices of both cultures made it even worse. The Jews rejected Samaritans and refused to acknowledge them as even partly Jewish.

In response, a cultural battle began as to which community was "truly" Jewish. Jerusalem was the cultural heart of the Jewish community and the location of their religious temple. The Samaritans, not to be outdone, built their temple on Mount Gerizim (where they claimed Abraham sacrificed Isaac) and called that the true center of worship (the woman at the well directly refers to this in John 4:20).

The culture war continued through the centuries and came to a head about two hundred years before this parable was taught. Between 175 to 163 BC, Antiochus IV Epiphanes declared himself the incarnation of the Greek god Zeus and mandated death to anyone who refused to worship him. The Jews refused, holding true to their beliefs. The Samaritans relented, however, and they repudiated all connection and kinship to the Jews and followed Antiochus.[1] In the eyes of the Jews, this destroyed any possibility of future reconciliation. The Samaritans were now dead to them.

As a result, both Jewish and Samaritan religious leaders taught that it was wrong to have any contact with the other group, and neither was to enter each other's territories or even speak to one another. The bitter hatred flowed in both directions.

Jesus knew how uncomfortable the historical pain was for both the Jews and Samaritans, and yet he intentionally evoked it. When he established the identity of the hero of the story as a Samaritan, he risked an adverse reaction strong enough to overshadow every other point he was making. Yet he did it anyway. Why?

In the strongest way possible, Jesus is creating a direct association between being a neighbor and being a reconciler. Faith, mission, and reconciliation have a deeply connected relationship with each other, and Jesus wants us to wrestle with the implications of that relationship.

The apostle Paul certainly did. Almost every one of his epistles has reconciliation as a dominant theme, and he saw reconciliation as one of the most natural expressions of life "in Christ" (see for example 2 Cor. 5:11–21; Gal. 3:28; Eph. 2:11–22; Col. 1:15–23). For Paul, being cemented to Jesus meant being a reconciler—period.

He clearly teaches this connection, found in 2 Corinthians 5:17–18: "Therefore, if anyone is *in Christ*, the new creation has come: The old has gone, the new is here! All this is from God, who reconciled us to himself through Christ and gave us the *ministry of reconciliation*" (emphasis added).

Reconciliation and being "in Christ" are intricately connected—anyone who is "in Christ" has been reconciled with God and is now a new creation. Because of the fact that we are reconciled with God, we have the confidence to boldly enter into the presence of God as sons and daughters of the Most High. But it goes beyond that—we are sent back into the world with the "ministry of reconciliation."

A phrase like that sounds beautiful, but it can often feel like grasping at clouds. What does it mean that we have been given the ministry of reconciliation?

Jesus brings it back to the real world with this parable in Luke 10. He gives a tangible expression of the ministry of reconciliation through the story of the good neighbor.

Put yourself in the shoes of his audience. They knew that Jews and Samaritans were forbidden to speak to each other. They knew the bitter history shared between these groups. So when the listening crowd heard that a Samaritan came upon a wounded Jew, how did they expect him to respond? They expected the Samaritan to walk right past the injured Jew. They probably expected him to gloat at his dire circumstances and attribute it to payback for centuries of animosity.

But in a shocking twist, the Samaritan does exactly the opposite. He demonstrates the heart of a reconciler and becomes the incarnation of a healer. He touches the man. He cares for him. He nurtures him. He finds provision for him.

It is a magnificent display of the ministry of reconciliation. It is a picture of a man who has been forgiven and who is able to extend forgiveness. It is a picture of someone who has experienced the love of God and who can in turn express the love of God in concrete and tangible ways.

I am particularly passionate about this aspect of being a neighbor because taking seriously the "mission of reconciliation" has had such a formative impact on my own life of faith. For much of my growing up years, and even into my early adulthood, reconciliation was not a theological concept that I ever had much exposure to. It wasn't until I was in my late twenties that I began to realize that reconciliation is not just a core expression of mission but is a core expression of Christianity itself.

Once I began to integrate the ministry of reconciliation into the way I thought about discipleship, new avenues opened up in my ability to experience God. The compassion (*splagchnizomai*) described earlier became real to me for the first time. I began to discover how it was that reconciliation could play a catalytic role in connecting my vision to God's vision.

Colossians 1:20 says that Jesus is reconciling all things to himself, and I used that as a platform for growing in my faith. I prayed that Jesus would begin to reveal some of the areas where his reconciliation power was at work in our day and age.

While in the midst of this journey, I asked Dr. John Perkins how we are to discern which area of the kingdom we are called to participate in with Jesus the reconciler. He responded by saying, "Look for the biggest issues of your day, and you will find Jesus there. I attacked the issues of my day. We dealt with racism and homelessness and housing and the breakdown of family. This is what kingdom leaders do. They identify the problems that cause suffering for the people, and they follow Jesus and work with the people who are affected by the problems to find solutions."

He was right. When our eyes begin to open to the big problems of society, we are well on our way to seeing the world as Jesus sees it and to getting in sync with the ministry of reconciliation that he is trying to share with us.

Asking Jesus to open my eyes to the big problems in our society was both a wonderful and overwhelming exercise. I began to see the incredible ways in which historical racism and poverty had created an unequal and unjust playing field within Chicago alone. I began to see how quickly a dangerous riptide could form when you mix together crime-ridden neighborhoods, failing schools, lack of employment, and a barren social support network. I began to deeply admire those who had somehow navigated and survived all of that, but I also mourned for the thousands who were still caught in the throes of it.

Little by little, through a process that I could only call faith, Jesus began to reveal to me how it was that I could be a neighbor who participated with him in the ministry of reconciliation. A number of important voices shaped that understanding within me, and I have tried to recognize many of them throughout my journey.

Dr. Marian Wright Edelman, the founder of the Children's Defense Fund,[2] is a devoted Christ follower, a passionate proponent of holistic faith, and one of the most inspiring people I have ever encountered. Her life vision is deeply informed by the passion with which Jesus often spoke about the need to care for and protect children. Matthew 18:6 is one of her favorite Bible passages: "If anyone causes one of these little ones—those who believe in me—to stumble, it would be better for them to have a large millstone hung around their neck and to be drowned in the depths of the sea."

She consistently advocates that in the spirit of Matthew 18, protecting children is one of the most tangible ways that we can be both a neighbor and a reconciler. She often reminds her listeners that children are the most vulnerable group within society and that the most vulnerable should be protected first. Furthermore, she says that the most dangerous place for the most vulnerable group in our country is at the intersection of race and poverty.

The precision of that language created a vivid picture for me, and in time I realized that one of the most substantial ways that I could contribute to the coming of the kingdom of God as a neighbor and reconciler would be to plant my life at the intersection of race and poverty. I would raise a family there, start a church there, and work closely with the families and neighborhood stakeholders who were already fighting for the abundant life of the children who lived at this intersection.

Dr. Wright Edelman has written a lot of great books, but my very favorite is *The Sea Is So Wide but My Boat Is So Small*. From that book comes this formative statement:

Powerful predators go after the weakest and the most vulnerable first. . . . Our children face so many dangers today from drug peddlers and gangs and pedophiles on the Internet and in institutions charged with protecting and educating them, and from guns and peers who lead them astray. Many poor children who are being sucked into a prison pipeline are bleeding from many wounds and face an accumulation of risks that overwhelm their fragile lives. Family dysfunction results in many children being sent into a broken and underfunded child welfare system, where they face multiple foster care placements and continuing instability. They attend failing schools that don't expect or help them to learn or to build their self-esteem. They live in violent, drug-saturated, and uncaring neighborhoods without health or mental health facilities or quality after-school, summer, and recreational programs. Congregations of faith dot almost as many inner city streets as liquor stores but, unlike liquor stores, their doors are often closed.[3]

When people meet me now, they know me only as the pastor of River City, and they assume that I have always lived the kind of life I have now. But when people from my earlier days interact with the current expression of my ministry, they struggle to understand how I got to where I am. When they see a church that has placed the "ministry of reconciliation" at the heart of its vision, and when they see how far I have moved out of my natural comfort zone, they are filled with questions. How did I develop such a burden for children who live at the intersection of race and poverty? How did I develop such a passion for justice and community development? How do I explain the voyage from a suburban, affluent, white church to an urban, multiethnic, economically diverse community?

I always give a one-word response, even though I know it's not what they are looking for: *faith*.

That might not seem like a legitimate answer to the question they are asking, but it is the only way I could possibly tell the story. Learning about faith is what pulled me past the boundaries of my fears. Learning about faith is what allowed me to go to new places in my intimate walk with God. Walking with God taught me about mission. Mission taught me about the kingdom of God. The kingdom of God taught me about the role of being a neighbor. Being a neighbor taught me about the centrality of reconciliation. Reconciliation brought me to the intersection of race and poverty, with a call to protect the children who live at that intersection.

For me, that's all wrapped around the single word *faith*.

That's what my hope is for you as well. When I share my own story, I am not suggesting it is the only or best way to be a neighbor. In fact, I trust that when you cement yourself to Jesus by faith, your story will end up looking quite a bit different from mine. I absolutely believe in the power of Ephesians 2:10, that "we are his workmanship, created in Christ Jesus for good works, which God prepared beforehand, that we should walk in them" (ESV).

I long for my fellow brothers and sisters who are trying to follow Christ with their lives to experience this richness of faith that catapults us toward action. I long for that knowledge of being Christ's workmanship to sink in so deeply that it can't be torn away by any trial or obstacle or fear that this life brings. That is what I wish for you. I want you to believe that this is true—that you are indeed Christ's workmanship. And I want you to be connected to Christ with life-giving, holistic, multidimensional faith. I wish for you to intimately walk with Christ, and then to walk into the good works that have already been prepared for you.

Trait 3: Justice—Rebuilding the Walls

At the end of his interaction with the law expert, Jesus asks him which of the three was the neighbor. Unable to acknowledge the humanity of the Samaritan, he simply replies, "The one who had mercy on him" (Luke 10:37). The word used for mercy is *eleos*, a derivative of the same word used in Micah 6:8: "He has shown you, O mortal, what is good. And what does the LORD require of you? To act justly and to love mercy and to walk humbly with your God."

Dr. Martin Luther King Jr. preached regularly on Luke 10, and you can find many of his sermons on the Good Samaritan online. Andrew Young, who was a civil rights leader, a United States congressman, mayor of Atlanta, and our nation's first African American ambassador to the United Nations, recounts a conversation he had with Dr. King on Luke 10. King told him,

Andy, I am tired of picking up people along the Jericho Road. I am
tired of seeing people battered and bruised and bloody, injured and
jumped on, along the Jericho Roads of life. This road is dangerous. I
don't want to pick up anyone else, along the Jericho Roads of life. . . .
I want to fix . . . the Jericho Road. I want to pave the Jericho Road,
add street lights to the Jericho Road; make the Jericho Road safe (for
passage) by everybody.[4]

This quote gives us a great picture of justice. Compassion helps us
to see as Jesus sees. Reconciliation moves us out of our comfort zones
and toward participating with the efforts of Jesus. Justice helps us
address the root causes that perpetually make the road a dangerous
place. Justice concerns itself with the systems and structures.

To use the words of Dr. King, justice is paving the Jericho Road,
adding streetlights, and making the Jericho Road safe for everybody.

///////////

After such a beautiful, comprehensive, and challenging story, Jesus
finds just the perfect words for ending the parable of the Good Samaritan. He has shown us the heart of God. He has shown us the
motivation of love and the holistic ways in which mission plays out.

Poetically, Jesus finishes with these simple but challenging words:
"Go and do likewise" (Luke 10:37).

20

////////////////////////

Fully Alive

I experienced the presence of the Divine as I had never experienced Him before. . . . Almost at once my fears began to go. . . . My uncertainty disappeared. I was ready to face anything.

Dr. Martin Luther King Jr.

It was close to midnight on January 27, 1956, and Dr. Martin Luther King Jr. was exhausted. In December 1955, Rosa Parks was arrested in Alabama for refusing to give up her seat at the front of the bus for a white man, and that became the match that lit the civil rights fire. A boycott was organized, and Dr. King was recruited to lead it. He initially had only lukewarm interest but ended up forming the Montgomery Improvement Association (MIA) with a group of other concerned citizens. The boycott to stop segregated busing was challenging but ultimately successful. The United States Supreme Court affirmed that the bus segregation laws of Montgomery were unconstitutional, the boycott ended, and Martin Luther King had become a national hero and an acknowledged leader in the civil rights struggle.

But the victory had not come without cost. King's life was now consistently in danger, and it was taking a psychological and spiritual toll on him. On this late night in January, his wife, Coretta, and his two-month-old daughter, Yolanda, were already asleep, and he was eager to join them.

Just before he got into bed, the phone rang. King grimaced, suspecting that he knew what awaited him if he chose to answer. For most people a middle of the night phone call would be unusual, but for the King family it was becoming too common. Threatening phone calls had become a daily reality for them. Afraid that the ringing would wake his family, King reluctantly answered. What he heard from the other end was as bad as he feared. One hateful insult after another was thrown at him in an attempt to tear apart his confidence. Once the long list of insults was finished, the caller ended the threat with a nasty finale. King was told that if he and his family didn't leave Montgomery immediately, they wouldn't live to see the end of the week.

Dr. King hung up without comment, as he had begun to do when receiving one of these disturbing calls. He had been able to ignore them for the most part, but something about this one cut all the way to the bone. Maybe it was the hatred that oozed from this particular caller. Maybe it was due to King's exhaustion. Maybe it was the sheer number of threats finally catching up to him.

He tried to calm himself down and decided to join his wife in bed. But as he lay there staring at the ceiling, anxiety began to take hold of him. He began to think of his precious daughter and her gentle smile. He began to think of his beautiful wife, who had sacrificed her music career so that he could take up leadership in the South. He began to wonder if the risk level was getting too high and feared that he might be putting his precious family in harm's way. What if they were taken away from him? Or more likely, what if he was taken from them?

The anxiety became overwhelming, and Dr. King realized he was not going to be able to fall asleep. He got up and headed to the kitchen to make a middle-of-the-night pot of coffee. He sat at the table and breathed deeply, trying to calm himself down. But like an incoming tide, the waves of fear and anxiety continued to rush in.

As the fear intensified that night, Dr. King began to entertain thoughts of resigning his post and stepping back from his important but dangerous mission. He began to develop an exit strategy in hopes that he could figure out "a way to move out of the picture without appearing a coward."[1]

As he sat at the kitchen table sipping the coffee, King's thoughts were interrupted by a sudden notion that at once intensified his desperation and clarified his options:

Something said to me, "You can't call on Daddy now, you can't call on Mama. You've got to call on that something in that person that your daddy used to tell you about, that power that can make a way out of no way."[2]

King was the son of a pastor, so prayer was a familiar practice in his home. But that night he discovered that different kinds of prayers are needed for different kinds of situations. There is a type of prayer that is sweet yet often superficial—a type of prayer where we ask God to bless us and keep us as we pursue our dreams. Then there is another type of prayer that comes from the deepest part of the soul—a prayer that is absolutely desperate for the power of God to intervene in a miraculous way. It was in this desperate place that Dr. King threw himself before God:

Lord, I'm down here trying to do what's right. I still think I'm right. I am here taking a stand for what I believe is right. But Lord, I must confess that I'm weak now, I'm faltering. I'm losing my courage. Now, I am afraid. And I can't let the people see me like this because if they see me weak and losing my courage, they will begin to get weak. The people are looking to me for leadership, and if I stand before them without strength and courage, they too will falter. I am at the end of my powers. I have nothing left. I've come to the point where I can't face it alone.[3]

King sat quiet, alone with his thoughts and prayers. He allowed the words of his petition to hang in the air for what seemed like forever. Suddenly, Dr. King sensed the presence of God begin to come near. He had a personal experience of Immanuel—"God with us." God began to speak to Dr. King's heart in a way that felt unmistakable:

Martin Luther, stand up for righteousness. Stand up for justice. Stand up for the truth. And lo, I will be with you. Even until the end of the world.[4]

Dr. King had come to God in desperation, and God had not let him down. God's grace, mercy, and love became so present, so tangible that King felt as if the resurrected Jesus was sitting right next to him. Dr. King felt Jesus speaking words of love, life, and courage to him, and he recorded those words in his journal:

> I heard the voice of Jesus saying still to fight on. He promised never to leave me, never to leave me alone. No never alone. No never alone. He promised never to leave me, never to leave me alone. . . . I experienced the presence of the Divine as I had never experienced Him before. . . . Almost at once my fears began to go. . . . My uncertainty disappeared. I was ready to face anything.[5]

As you and I learn to respond to the voice of Jesus and go out in faith, it is unlikely that we will ever face a threat as ominous as that which Dr. King faced. Our lives will probably never be on the line as we carry out a missional task from God. But whether it's an extraordinary assignment like leading the civil rights movement or a seemingly ordinary assignment like me searching for disconnected people at Axis, the pathway to vibrant, transformational faith remains the same for every follower of Jesus.

To become fully alive in Jesus, a Christ follower needs to learn to embrace all three dimensions of faith: faith and fear, faith and intimacy, and faith and mission.

Dr. King's most significant faith encounter began at the same intersection as the faith leaders throughout the corridors of history: faith and fear. I am thankful that he did not attempt to portray his walk of faith as one that was absent of fear. It was just the opposite—he met Jesus most profoundly at this very intersection. The sound bites of fear from his journal are a powerful reminder that fear is not a sign of weakness—it is the precondition of courage. Courage is not required until fear has emerged as a serious threat to immobilize your progress.

This was also true for Joshua, my biblical prototype for holistic, multidimensional faith. God offered Joshua the entrustment of a significant mission. But if Joshua was going to have the courage to follow in faith, he was first going to need to identify and overcome his fear. That is where his faith journey kicked into the next level. Once he acknowledged the anxiety that came from the loss of his mentor Moses, he was poised to courageously fall into the providential arms of God. Faith-based courage was the only way through the maze of fear.

This was true for the original disciples of Jesus. In order to respond to the call, "Follow me," they had to first overcome their fear. In order to follow Jesus into dangerous and risky environments, they had to first overcome their fear. In order for Peter to boldly step toward Jesus in the water, he had to first overcome his fear.

This has been true for me at every step of my faith journey. Every significant era of growth has been preceded by an encounter with Jesus at the intersection of fear and faith. Each time I come to that intersection, I have to once again make a decision. Will I retreat toward that which represents the illusion of safety and security? Or will I step toward Jesus in faith, trusting that he will make clear a path where a path does not yet seem to exist?

The only way to truly defeat fear in your life is to take heed of the words and imagery of the writer of Hebrews. No other writer in the Bible spent as much of his letter teaching on faith as he did, and this was at the center of his understanding:

> Therefore, since we are surrounded by such a great cloud of witnesses, let us throw off everything that hinders and the sin that so easily entangles. And let us run with perseverance the race marked out for us, fixing our eyes on Jesus, the pioneer [or author] and perfecter of faith. (Heb. 12:1–2)

If you desire to be transformed through faith in a daily, interactive relationship with Jesus, then this is the secret. This is where the courage to overcome our fears finds its source. We fix our eyes on Jesus, the author, pioneer, and perfecter of our faith.

When we live like this—with our eyes fixed on Jesus—we not only overcome fear but also begin to experience incredible intimacy with God. Jesus meets us at our point of insecurity and anxiety and speaks transformational words of warmth, comfort, and assurance of his presence to the deepest parts of our soul.

That is what kept Dr. Martin Luther King Jr. moving forward. He was filled with fear, but the intimacy that came from the nearness of Jesus was ultimately more powerful: "I heard the voice of Jesus. . . . He promised never to leave me, never to leave me alone. . . . Almost at once my fears began to go . . . My uncertainty disappeared. I was ready to face anything."[6]

That is what intimacy with God does for a human being. Following Jesus in faith doesn't mean you live without fear. Following Jesus in faith means that the fear you feel begins to lose its grip on you. You feel Jesus near, you hear his reassuring voice, and you become filled with a force even more powerful than fear.

The apostle John understood this. Meditating on the reality of Jesus, he shared these words: "You, dear children, are from God and have overcome them, because the one who is in you is greater than the one who is in the world" (1 John 4:4).

Dr. King understood this as well. He heard Jesus reassure him, promising never to leave him and never to leave him alone. That promise of intimacy was what helped Dr. King's uncertainty to disappear and allowed his courage to grow.

This was the fuel of faith for Joshua as well: "As I was with Moses, so I will be with you; I will never leave you nor forsake you. . . . Be strong and courageous. Do not be afraid; do not be discouraged, for the LORD your God will be with you wherever you go" (Josh. 1:5, 9).

Intimacy with Jesus is the center of Christian faith. It helps us overcome fear, and it prepares us to step into courageous mission. The words of Jesus become both our motivation and our guide. Joshua became filled with faith-based courage to step forward into his mission. Dr. King heard these words from Jesus, and they echo the words of faith that God has spoken to men and women of faith throughout the course of history: "Martin Luther, stand up for righteousness. Stand up for justice. Stand up for the truth. And lo, I will be with you. Even until the end of the world."[7]

The words that Dr. King heard from Jesus that night echoed the words that the disciples heard from the risen Jesus as they were sent on mission: "All authority in heaven and on earth has been given to me. Therefore go and make disciples of all nations, baptizing them in the name of the Father and of the Son and of the Holy Spirit, and teaching them to obey everything I have commanded you. And surely I am with you always, to the very end of the age" (Matt. 28:18–20).

In the King James Version the last part of that sounds like this: "And lo, I am with you always, even unto the end of the world." Sounds just like what Dr. King heard, doesn't it?

My hope is that this book has helped stir a longing within you to live with this kind of faith. My hope is that you will embrace the reality that being fully alive is not as much a result of something we do as a result of placing our faith in Jesus. My hope is that you will gain a vision for a holistic, multidimensional faith and that you will be inspired by the possibility of all three dimensions of faith operating in your life at the same time.

When we have experiences of faith like this, we begin to be connected to the promise of abundant life in Jesus. When we live like this, the sense that something is missing disappears and the reality of a vibrant, interactive life of faith in Jesus replaces that void. When we live like this, we embody the words of Saint Irenaeus: "The glory of God is a human being fully alive."

Notes

Chapter 2: Something's Missing

1. James Cone, *A Black Liberation of Theology* (Maryknoll, NY: Orbis Books, 2011), 50–51.

Chapter 3: People of the Story

1. Dr. Klyne Snodgrass gave this lecture at River City Community Church on July 9, 2012. A podcast is available at https://itunes.apple.com/podcast/river-city-community -church/id218083547?mt=2.

2. Depending on how some of these verses are translated, Dr. Snodgrass says it can also appear in English as "in the Lord," "in him," or "in whom."

3. Martin Luther, *Luther's Works, Vol. 26: Lectures on Galatians Chapters 1–4* (St. Louis: Concordia, 1962), 168.

Chapter 4 Faith in 3-D

1. Luther, *Luther's Works*, 168.

2. *Wikipedia*, s.v. "prototype," last modified October 9, 2013, http://en.wikipedia. org/wiki/Prototype.

Chapter 6: Boundary Breaking

1. Gary Haugen, *Just Courage: God's Great Expedition for the Restless Christian* (Downers Grove, IL: InterVarsity, 2008), 146.

2. Brennan Manning, *The Ragamuffin Gospel* (Colorado Springs: Multnomah, 1990), 49.

Chapter 7: Sink or Swim

1. John Perkins, *With Justice for All: A Strategy for Community Development* (Ventura, CA: Regal, 2011), 49.

Chapter 8: Safe or Brave

1. Haugen, *Just Courage*, 113.

Chapter 9: Pay Attention

1. Dr. Martin Luther King Jr., *A Testament of Hope: The Essential Writings and Speeches of Martin Luther King, Jr.*, ed. James M. Washington (1986; repr. ed., New York, HarperOne, 2003), 511.
2. Ibid., emphasis added.
3. Dictionary.com, s.v. "harness," accessed October 3, 2013.

Chapter 11: The Garden

1. C. S. Lewis, *The Screwtape Letters* (New York: HarperCollins, 2009), 3.
2. C. S. Lewis, *Mere Christianity* (New York: HarperCollins, 2001), 47–48.

Chapter 13: The Butterfly Effect

1. A. W. Tozer, *The Knowledge of the Holy* (New York: HarperCollins, 1978), 1.

Chapter 14: Pleasing God

1. Richard Rohr, *Richard Rohr's Daily Meditations* (daily email), April 13, 2011; adapted from *Following the Mystics Through the Narrow Gate . . . Seeing God in All Things* (CD, DVD, MP3).
2. Willard builds his philosophy of spiritual transformation around the acronym VIM, which I have found to be very helpful. VIM stands for *Vision, Intent*, and *Means*. See chap. 5 of his book *Renovation of the Heart* (Colorado Springs: NavPress, 2011), 77–82.

Chapter 17: Kingdom People

1. Dallas Willard, *Knowing Christ Today* (New York: HarperCollins, 2009), 150.

Chapter 19: Neighbors

1. For a basic overview of the history of the Samaritans, see http://en.wikipedia.org/wiki/Samaritans.
2. Children's Defense Fund is a nonprofit child advocacy organization dedicated to protecting children. See http://www.childrensdefense.org for more info.
3. Dr. Marian Wright Edelman, *The Sea Is So Wide and My Boat Is So Small* (New York: Hyperion, 2008), 35.
4. John Hope Bryant, "Fixing the Jerico Road," *Huffington Post*, January 13, 2010, http://www.huffingtonpost.com/john-hope-bryant/fixing-the-jericho-road_b_422612.html.

Chapter 20: Fully Alive

1. Clayborne Carson, ed., *The Autobiography of Martin Luther King, Jr.* (New York: Grand Central Publishing, 2001), 77.
2. Ibid.
3. Ibid.
4. Ibid., 78.
5. Ibid.
6. Ibid.
7. Ibid.

Daniel Hill is the founding and senior pastor of River City Community Church, located in the Humboldt Park neighborhood of Chicago. The vision of River City is centered around the core values of worship, reconciliation, and neighborhood development. Formed in 2003, River City longs to see increased spiritual renewal as well as social and economic justice in the Humboldt Park neighborhood and entire city, demonstrating compassion and alleviating poverty as tangible expressions of the kingdom of God.

Prior to starting River City, Daniel launched a dot-com in the 1990s before serving for five years on the staff of Willow Creek Community Church in the suburbs of Chicago. Daniel holds a BS in business from Purdue University, an MA in theology from Moody Bible Institute, and a certificate in church-based community and economic development from Harvard Divinity School, and he is currently pursuing his DMin in community development at Northern Seminary. Daniel and his wife, Elizabeth, who is a professor of psychology at Chicago State University, are the proud parents of Xander and Gabriella Hill.

"A lot of folks tiptoe through life just to arrive at death safely, coming to die only to find that they have not truly lived. Daniel Hill's debut book is a manifesto of life—an invitation to look our fears in the face and live in defiance of them. It is a celebration of the God who came to give life—not death or religion or fluff or guilt, but life. Hallelujah!"

—**Shane Claiborne**, activist; bestselling author

"I've known Daniel for fifteen years. When you spend time with him, you find his bravery and passion contagious, and just the same thing happened to me as I read these pages. His message is intelligent, courageous, and necessary."

—**Shauna Niequist**, author of *Bread & Wine*

"Jesus told his disciples to observe his way of life and to then follow that pattern by faithfully living out these same actions in our everyday lives. What we need is a holistic vision of Christian discipleship that returns us to that essence of who Jesus was and what he taught his followers to do. In *10:10* we get a vision of that wholeness of life in Christ and a path that leads us to becoming a holistic witness for God."

—**Dr. John Perkins**, bestselling author; cofounder of the Christian Community Development Association

"Daniel Hill has the uncanny ability to bring us from what can seem a routine or lifeless faith and understanding of God to something very vivid, colorful, and anything but routine. If you wonder if you are missing something in your walk with God but can't understand what it might be, *10:10* will help you identify that and jump-start you back to the place you are meant to be."

—**Dan Kimball**, author of *Adventures in Churchland: Finding Jesus in the Mess of Organized Religion*

"Many lament the decline in church and religion as we've known them. But Daniel Hill believes church and religion as we've known them must make way for something better. He invites us to join him as pioneers in search of 'something better'—to cross the frontier of fear and discover, on the other side, what it means to be fully alive."

—**Brian D. McLaren**, author; speaker; activist

"Daniel Hill provides a biblical and prophetic vision for a holistic ministry of faith in the complex world of North American churches. He asks the difficult but essential questions that all Christians need to ask. Daniel Hill's life and ministry, and now this book, testify to how faith leads to the fullness of life found in the mission of God."

—**Dr. Soong-Chan Rah**, author; Milton B. Engebretson Associate Professor of Church Growth and Evangelism at North Park Seminary

"If you're looking for a book that gives full measure to the fullness of life in Christ, Daniel Hill has written it. Don't leave the bookstore without this book, and take enough to share the full measure of the pleasure with other disciples."

—**Leonard Sweet**, bestselling author; professor at Drew University and George Fox University; chief contributor to Sermons.com

"Daniel Hill compels and challenges us to live life to the fullest extent that God has designed for us. This book is a personal, theological, and activistic approach to our faith that stirs deeply and pushes us all toward a more vibrant life."

—**Heather Larson**, executive pastor of Willow Creek Community Church

"In a consumer culture it is difficult to rescue the term *abundance* from the idea of more stuff. It is even more challenging to bring the deep language Jesus uses when he talks about abundance into our culture in a way that makes sense and creates freedom. Daniel Hill does that, and he has given us a book that creates a stirring in hearts that have an abundance of things but an emptiness of spirit. A much-needed book."

—**Rick McKinley**, author; pastor of Imago Dei Community, Portland, OR

"Caution! This book has the potential to ignite a faith movement among the next generation of Christ followers that will release their unrealized potential and transform communities around the world. I highly recommend it!"

—**Rev. Dr. Brenda Salter McNeil**, speaker; author; professor of reconciliation studies at Seattle Pacific University

"Reading Daniel Hill's new book, it is clear he understands the challenges of being sold out to faith in Jesus in the real world full of conflict, confusion, and compromise. I feel encouraged that in spite of my limitations, I can lean into the abundant life Daniel encourages us to embrace."

—**Noel Castellanos**, CEO of the Christian Community Development Association

"Through faith, word, and action, Daniel Hill has lived into his calling as a young, urban pastor of a dynamic, multiethnic church. Now he shares the challenges faced, principles employed, and lessons learned as he has grown into his role. More than a collection of clever formulas and hip anecdotes, *10:10* comes from the heart of a pastor who is passionate about seeing holistic faith translated into every aspect of life and ministry. Daniel's book is a gift to Christian leaders in need of encouragement and a fresh vision."

—**Edward Gilbreath**, author of *Birmingham Revolution* and *Reconciliation Blues*

"Daniel Hill is a man of faith. He has lived out his faith in the context of the inner city where his faith has been tested on a daily basis. Daniel, along with his wife and children, has taken the challenge to live in a place of difficulties with people who are often neglected and have been pushed to the margins of society. They have needed a strong and vibrant faith to survive. Who better than Daniel to teach us about faith? His book *10:10* details how faith is the path to live life in its fullness. I wholeheartedly recommend this book for any person on the course of knowing and living for Christ."

—**Wayne Gordon**, author; cofounder of CCDA;
pastor of Lawndale Christian Community Church

"Our faith is too small. We have an infinite God, but we don't realize what that can mean for our lives. Daniel Hill is living faith in its fullness, and he calls us to do the same. It is a God call, a transformative call, a truly biblical call, a call to a life beyond your dreams. Learn how to truly trust God and live a life full of adventure. And watch the blessings that are poured out upon the people."

—**Michael O. Emerson**, author; Allyn and Gladys Cline Professor
of Sociology and co-director of the Kinder Institute
for Urban Research at Rice University

"In *10:10*, Daniel Hill reminds us of the life we have in Jesus Christ. Informed by his incredible life of service and leadership, Daniel explores the full force faith can and ought to have in our lives. *10:10* is in the tradition of the best of Dallas Willard's writing: insistent on the power available to Christ followers in the here and now. *10:10* will reinvigorate your faith and call you deeper into the abundant life Daniel so passionately describes in this moving book."

—**Michael Wear**, writer; speaker; founding partner of Values
Partnerships; former National Faith Vote Director
for the White House's faith-based initiative

"In *10:10,* Daniel Hill invites us to an applied faith, fully submitting our lives to Jesus. With thoughtful analysis of Scripture and real-life examples, Daniel provides a pathway toward the abundant life to which Christ invites his followers."

—**Matthew Soerens**, author;
field director for Evangelical Immigration Table

"So many of us live life in black and white, when Jesus offers us life in full color and high definition. Daniel helps us access what is right in front of us yet seemingly so far away: God's peace, presence, and power. Tired of the status quo? Experience *10:10: Life to the Fullest!*"

—**Dr. Eric Michael Bryant**, pastor at Gateway Church, Austin;
author of *Not Like Me: A Field Guide
for Influencing a Diverse World*